TRUE BALANCE

Also by Sonia Choquette

The Psychic Pathway
Your Heart's Desire
The Wise Child

TRUE BALANCE

A Commonsense Guide for
Renewing Your Spirit

SONIA CHOQUETTE, PH.D.

Three Rivers Press
New York

Published by Three Rivers Press, New York, New York.
Member of the Crown Publishing Group.

Random House, Inc. New York, Toronto, London, Sydney, Auckland
www.randomhouse.com

Three Rivers Press is a registered trademark and the Three Rivers Press colophon is a trademark of Random House, Inc.

Printed in the United States of America

Design by Jan Derevjanik

Library of Congress Cataloging-in-Publication Data
   Choquette, Sonia.
      True balance : a creative guide for chakra well-being / Sonia Choquette. — 1st pbk. ed.
      1. Chakras.   I. Title.
   BF1442.C53 C46 2000
   131—dc21   99-059793

ISBN 0-609-80398-0

10 9 8 7 6 5

To my family
You balance my soul

Acknowledgments

I would like to thank my parents, Sonia and Paul, for giving me a solid and lasting foundation. You welcomed me into the world and let me know the Universe would always support me.

To my dear husband, partner, and playmate, Patrick Tully: Thank you for awakening my vitality and showering me with nurturing, sensuality, and romance. Life with you has been the sweetest adventure.

To my coach, Anne Simon Wolf: Thank you for helping me reclaim my sovereignty and become "Queen" in my universe.

To my sweet children, Sonia and Sabrina: Thank you for opening my heart and teaching me how to love unconditionally.

To my sister Cuky: Thank you for listening to me when I needed support and for singing in bed with me every night when we were growing up. You have always championed my expression.

To my mentors, LuAnn Glatzmaier and Joan Smith: Thank you for opening my eyes and helping me to see the wonder and beauty of the Universe.

To Divine Spirit, Holy Mother-Father God: I am humbly and deeply grateful for all the blessings and gifts you continue to shower upon me and my loved ones every day. I am forever your servant.

I would also like to thank my agent and ally, Susan Schulman, for clearing the way to my heart's desire as a writer and a teacher. You have continually provided the highest venue for my dreams.

To Annetta Hanna, my editor: Thank you for challenging me to become a better teacher and writer. Your input has been a tremendous help to me on both a personal and professional basis.

To Lauren Shakely, Chip Gibson, Tina Constable, Leigh Ann Ambrosi, and all the behind-the-scenes contributors at Crown Publishing: Thank you for providing a wonderful home to all of my books and for the continued enthusiasm and support in each and every project.

To my teachers, Charlie Goodman and Dr. Trenton Tully: Thank you for ushering me onto my path in this life. You opened my heart and mind to Divine wisdom.

To Debra Grace Graves and Kimo, the kahuna: Thank you for helping me bring this book into the world.

To my clients and students, who continue to be my best teachers: I honor and appreciate you from the deepest place in my soul. Thank you for allowing me to know you so intimately and to learn from you so much.

Contents

Introduction

Recently I had an urgent telephone message on my answering machine from a man named Steven, saying, "Sonia, you don't know me, but I was referred to you by my massage therapist. I went to see her because I've been feeling extremely drained and overwhelmed lately, and nothing in my life is going smoothly. She told me it's because my chakras are out of balance. She tried to explain to me that chakras are energy centers that we all have, but honestly I didn't understand what she meant. Finally she referred me to you and said you could help! So can you? I need to know what these energy centers are and how to get them to stop messing up my life!"

Receiving Steven's call was not surprising. In the past few years, I've had many phone calls just like his, each one requesting guidance through one energy crisis after another. More and more people are discovering that what ails them is more psychic and spiritual in nature than physical. Steven, like many of my clients, had never even heard of the energy centers called *chakras*. To him, it was no more than a curious word, maybe a metaphor, but certainly not something that was intrinsic to his nature and essential to his overall well-being. He couldn't imagine that an invisible energy center, a chakra, could have anything to do with his problems, and in fact he laughed at the idea when it was suggested. But the truth is, his massage therapist was right. Most of our problems can be traced to one or more of our seven psychic energy centers, known to the metaphysically savvy as chakras, from the Hindi term meaning "spinning wheel," which from an energetic perspective is what a chakra would actually look like.

Here in the West, we think of ourselves as solid bodies, but Eastern thinking correctly perceives us being more ethereal. When Hindus visualize a human being, they visualize our seven separate but interconnected centers of energy, each maintaining a certain center of human well-being. To the rational Western mind, the idea of such energy centers seems farfetched, yet our own language accurately reflects our instinctive awareness of these psychic centers. We say, for example:

- "He's a pain in the neck," of someone who affects our throat chakra by making us speechless with rage

- "She galls me," of the coworker who affects our third chakra by overriding our authority and ignoring our decisions

- "He knocks me off my feet," of the new lover who overwhelms our routine and threatens our first chakra, our foundation, causing us to feel ungrounded.

Our energy system governs our energetic and psychic well-being. This system includes our foundation and survival instincts, our vitality and emotional sensations, our will and personal sovereignty, our ability to give and receive love, our creative expression, our psychic awareness and personal vision, and our capacity to connect with our Creator. It is the matrix that channels our spirit into our body and allows us to express ourselves freely on the physical plane. When these seven centers of energy are balanced, we feel grounded, emotionally safe, mentally in charge, receptive to love and loving, effective and creative in all forms of our expression, inspired and imaginative, and intimately connected to and guided by the Universe. This is the natural plan for human experience. Such a life is exciting, satisfying, productive, and fulfilling and allows us to channel our best into the planet. It is a life lived as the Universe intends. It is a life filled with love, creativity, and blessings.

But when one or more of these seven chakras falls out of balance or fails to operate as it is designed to, essential parts of our psychic and spiritual expression become dysfunctional or shut down. When this happens, we become insecure or feel threatened in the world. We fall out of communion with our emotions and fail to interpret their messages correctly. We find ourselves operating out of fear, with a reduced capacity to give and receive love. We lose touch with our integrity and begin to express other than what is in our hearts, coming to doubt ourselves, or deny our value and importance. We lose our capacity to see the truth in ourselves and in the world, and in the worst case, we become disconnected from our source, God. Such a life becomes an overwhelming attempt to avoid death rather than experience each day. It is a life filled with anxiety, terror, isolation, anger, dishonesty, manipulation, and loneliness. It is a sad and wasteful loss both to us and to the world, for in this condition we are unable to bring our gifts to the world and make our unique and essential contribution to the whole. We suffer, and the world suffers as well.

As an intuitive and healer, my fundamental task is to help people understand their spiritual anatomy. I teach about these energy centers and show people how to stay balanced and psychically aligned so that they can fully participate in the natural plan. When I consult with clients, I am able to discern intuitively which of their energy centers are out of balance and, more important, why and what to do about it. I teach my clients and readers how to perceive and appreciate themselves as delicate, responsive energetic beings who require the same care and attention as any other creation in nature. Like flowers and plants, we too need ground under our feet, warmth and sunshine and food for our spirit, protective boundaries, tending and care, freedom to grow unencumbered and without limitation, and complete support from the Universe to become our greatest possible self.

Because the modern world has failed to recognize that we are spiritual beings, with basic requirements for maintaining spiritual as well as physical health, it is no wonder that so many of us struggle with diseases and disruptions of the spirit. When we ignore what we need to keep our spirit in balance, we suffer the consequences.

When we fall into doubt about our basic energetic rights and fail to meet our basic psychic needs, we wither and languish. Like an unwatered potted plant, neglected in the corner, we may manage to survive, but we will hardly reach our full potential to flower and contribute to the world. Such a life is lived in pain. And such pain is unnecessary. The entire Universe is organized around our well-being. We are naturally and intrinsically designed through our energetic body to freely receive all that our spirits need in order to thrive. Our job is to learn about our energy body and how to keep it in working order. And for over thirty years, it has been my job to teach this essential course in spiritual and psychic well-being.

After my conversation with Steven, a seed was planted in my mind. What people like him needed, I realized, was a practical, commonsense guide for understanding their chakra system and keeping it in balance.

Consequently, I decided to write this book, explaining how our energy centers operate and how we can keep them running smoothly. Because I've counseled so many people over the years, I have also come to recognize what people in our time-crunched society are able to do in order to take better spiritual care of themselves. I've therefore created an easy-to-use workbook that describes each of the seven energy centers, both balanced and imbalanced, and offers practical ways for rebalancing our lives.

You can refer to this workbook whenever you are feeling out of sorts or are in need of a psychic "tune-up." I've intentionally included a variety of rebalancing suggestions that speak to every mood and temperament. They are not to be interpreted as more assignments to add to your endless "to do" list, but rather as simple practices that require minimum attention while bringing about maximum relief. Try one or all of them, depending on your mood and your personality. Use the ideas that appeal to you, and ignore the others. Some suggestions may feel right one day and not the next. That is the nature of the energy body. Because it is in a constant state of flux, you need to experiment with the remedies to discover which ones work for you. Besides, variety is the spice of life. Once you begin to appreciate what the different energy centers need in order to be balanced, don't be surprised if you find yourself coming up with your own remedies for restoring psychic equilibrium!

GETTING STARTED

Before you begin, I suggest you read through the entire book first, making notes in the sections that speak to you. Then go back and reread the specific sections that address the problems you are experiencing. Normally our energy system builds one level upon another. When one chakra becomes imbalanced, it will tend to throw the chakras surrounding it off balance as well, just as one imbalanced wheel on a car will throw off the others. It is important to note, however, that some of your seven energy centers may be working just fine while others are sluggish or imbalanced. For example, a person with a strong personality may have a well-balanced third chakra, or sense of direction, yet have an imbalanced fifth chakra, or center for expression. Such a person may then come off sounding bossy or overbearing, creating problems for himself. Someone else with a great imagination may have a very well-balanced sixth chakra, or sense of vision, but be weak in the first chakra, or sense of foundation, thus creating frustration and ineffectiveness in getting her ideas manifested.

Generally you will want to balance your energy centers or chakras one at a time, starting with the first and moving up to the seventh. But if one imbalanced energy center is clearly causing you difficulty, balance that center immediately and then go back and tune up the others. You may want to work on more than one energy center at a time—balancing the second and third simultaneously, for example. If you find, however, that you are working on more than three chakras at a time, I suggest that you stop what you are doing and go back to the beginning, balancing your first chakra and then working upward.

As you approach this work, think of it as preventive medicine for the spirit. Ideally, this book will educate you on how to maintain your subtle psychic body with intelligence and ease. Once you understand how your energy centers work and what it takes to keep them running smoothly, you will be able to stabilize your energy and nurture yourself body, mind, and soul. Then if you experience any psychic difficulty, you will require only a quick reminder to address the problem.

When you balance your chakras, you reclaim your natural rights and reestablish your natural order. You begin to undo the damage that was caused by living your life backward, from the head first, forgetting the body and spirit altogether. As with everything in nature, if your life isn't supported by a grounded source of energy, it will wither and lose its vitality. As you learn about the chakras, you will discover that balancing them isn't particularly hard, especially if you think of it as a process of not just living your life, but actually *loving* your life!

In honoring your right to all that you require to grow and thrive, I hope this book will serve as a supportive and handy manual. Keep it by your bedside or in a drawer at work, and refer to it whenever you need a solution for your psychic disturbances or tips for preserving your balance.

I believe the most profound gift you can offer to those you love and to the world at large is to be a happy, whole, and balanced being. You then become a light-bearer in the world, a natural expression of God's beauty, and a model of health and vitality for those who are still struggling in the dark. When your chakras are psychically balanced, you will find that the guidance you require for healing, light, and inner peace comes naturally. This is the Divine plan and is as the Universe intends it to be. So in reclaiming your right to such spiritual alignment, let the balancing act begin!

OUR PERSONAL POWER and well-being originate in the first chakra. This center, situated in the energy field at the base of the tailbone, welcomes our spirit into our body and creates the necessary foundation with which we can begin life's journey. Activated at birth when the umbilical cord is cut, it channels the life force into our physical body, concentrating its flow on the area from the tailbone down through the feet, helping us establish our footing and take our place in the world. The moment we are born, we are released from our mother's support system and simultaneously hooked into this spiritual source of supply. It establishes our personal access to all that we need in order to survive and grow, providing us with a basic sense of security and safety. It empowers us with the intuitive understanding that we are children of the Universe with the right to grow into our fullest expression in this lifetime. On the color spectrum, this chakra vibrates energetically to the color red.

When our first chakra is balanced, our foundation becomes well rooted. We will feel as if we have been

First Chakra

Balanced Foundation

invited to the banquet of life as honored guests. Life is welcoming, ready to embrace us and offer us support and nurturance in every way. We intuitively trust that no matter where we find ourselves, life will be generous in offering us endless opportunities with which to meet our basic needs. With a well-established psychic foundation, we feel that not only is life a party, the party is for us.

Our first chakra's primary function is to assist us in meeting our basic needs for survival gracefully and with ease. Its mission statement is "I want, I need, give me, give me now!" It focuses our attention on what we need day to day in order to survive, and it stimulates our ability to reach out for and demand fulfillment. A balanced foundation allows us to feel confident in the belief that the Universe will collaborate with us in meeting our requirements to grow and thrive in this life. It keeps us from internalizing the chaos of the world and helps us refrain from joining the chorus of "I can't, I won't, I'm afraid," from which so many people suffer. It supports us in staying connected to our true spiritual heritage and creates a sense of belonging, of feeling wanted, of being a part of the community and of feeling worthy and worthwhile. One of my favorite images for a balanced foundation is that of a plant or tree rooted firmly in the ground, solidly supported by Mother Earth.

GROUNDED AND CALM

On a practical level, the first chakra governs our desire to eat, to have shelter, warmth, and comfort, and to be protected from the hostile elements of the world. In the actual physical body, it governs the bones, the blood, the immune system, the colon, the rectum, the legs, and the feet. When you are not balanced in the first chakra, you may have difficulties with these areas of your body.

An open and balanced foundation gives you a solid sense of security that is deeply felt and fundamentally comforting. You can always tell if you have a well-balanced foundation by the simple fact that you don't worry much. You seem to inherently expect the best from life, and you usually get it. Perhaps you know someone with a well-balanced first chakra. It may be a loved infant who makes cranky demands and expects them to be fulfilled without a second thought, or it may be your "lucky" friend who seems to attract to herself everything she wants. It may even be the quietly secure little old lady who lives next door, always smiling and optimistic, never worried about the future. Ideally it will be you. No matter whether they are young or old, people with a well-balanced foundation intuitively expect that whatever they need, they will have. With a grounded foundation, you will be calm and easygoing and have an aura of quiet strength and confidence about you. You will also be reassuring to be around. When your foundation is strong, you do not rush toward life. Instead you know that life will move toward you, meeting you in the middle. And it does.

LOOKING AT YOUR OWN FOUNDATION

Are you confident in knowing you will have all that you need?

_____

Do you ever worry about your survival?

_____

Can you say that you feel grounded?

_____

Do you know anyone who is grounded?

_____

How would you describe the energy of a grounded person?

_____

AN IMBALANCED FOUNDATION

If your first chakra is weak or off balance, you will not feel grounded and secure. Rather than feeling like a solidly rooted tree in the forest, standing strong and well supported, you will more likely feel like a cut flower in a vase, vulnerable, threatened, even doomed. You may unconsciously feel that you draw from a diminishing or limited supply of resources. You may fall into a fearful state of existence.

An imbalanced or weakened foundation leaves a person insecure and anxious, struggling with feelings ranging from mild uneasiness to full-blown paranoia. People who do not have a well-grounded foundation or root chakra find it a tremendous struggle to meet life's basic needs. They often worry that they are not entitled to the things in life that allow them to feel secure, such as a warm home, financial security, and safe emotional connections with others.

Sometimes, in an attempt to correct a weak foundation, a person can overcompensate, causing their first chakra to become overactive. If this occurs, your focus on survival will become exaggerated, leaving you feeling as though everything potentially threatens your sense of safety and support. You become aggressive in your efforts to take care of yourself. Not surprisingly, this painful state causes one to assume a "me first" attitude and become pushy, manipulative, greedy, or insensitive to others in order to survive, taking what you can when you can, no matter what.

I had a client named Alice who had a very overactive first chakra. She was the sixth in a family of nine children. During her childhood, she was highly competitive with her siblings, having to fight with them to get anything she needed, from supper, to privacy in the bathroom, to the attention of her parents. Because she grew up in such a constant state of deprivation, her attitude became one of "I'm going to survive no matter what! I'm going to grab what I can and run!" Her dog-eat-dog attitude led to a total disconnection with everyone around her. Feeling so psychically threatened and deprived clouded her perspective on everything. Supply, in her view, was limited. She truly believed there was not enough in the world to go around; somebody was going to lose, and if she could help it, it certainly wasn't going to be her! This belief made her desperate, greedy, selfish, and obnoxious.

The irony was that though she had no real friends, Alice's aggressive personality had created in her life a very abundant flow of money. Unfortunately, though she was quite well off, she couldn't feel it. Instead she experienced life as an endless struggle, fierce with obstacles, forever requiring her to dodge threats and looming poverty. In spite of her defensive and aloof outward demeanor, deep down Alice was actually very scared and insecure. She didn't feel at all comforted by her prosperity, and because of her behavior, she instinctively knew people didn't like her, making her feel even more isolated and lonely. Hers was a very sad and painful existence, one that no one deserves. Eventually she decided to seek help.

It took Alice a long while and a major reeducation to learn about her foundation and discover how to balance it. She did so by entering group therapy as well as receiving personal one-on-one counseling. She also joined a progressive church that offered many classes on abundance and faith. She began to make a few friends and managed to step back from her many day-to-day skirmishes. Aware that her problems were more psychic and energetic in nature than based in reality, she maintained a constant vigilance over her negative beliefs so that she wouldn't fall back into her old aggressive mode. Her efforts paid off. She began to relax and trust that she would be safe and comfortable in the world. For once, she actually began to enjoy her life.

Telltale signs of an imbalanced first chakra are nagging and persistent psychic insecurities and anxieties, especially those centered on your basic survival, security, safety, and support needs. If you worry excessively about money and security, especially when you have adequate financial means, you have an imbalanced foundation. Other signs of imbalance are failing to connect with others, feeling isolated and self-conscious, having no sense of community, being unreasonably suspicious of others, and feeling that the world is not a safe place. Symptoms include nervousness, anxiety, feelings of abandonment, and most of all, worry, worry, worry. An imbalanced first chakra leaves you feeling unwelcome, unworthy, unwanted, and afraid.

Whether over- or underactive, an imbalanced foundation creates fear and preoccupation offering protection from what seems like a hostile, scarce, and unwelcoming world. Life lived from that frame of mind is actually very painful and frightening—yet such pain and fear are unnecessary.

CHECKING YOUR FOUNDATION

	Yes	No	Sometimes
Do you feel anxious, overly concerned with survival?	_____	_____	_____
Fearful, not sure-footed in the world?	_____	_____	_____
Worried, scared that you can't handle life?	_____	_____	_____
Threatened, afraid something terrible will occur at any moment?	_____	_____	_____
Insecure or inadequate?	_____	_____	_____
Isolated, like you don't fit in, don't belong?	_____	_____	_____
Suspicious, thinking the worst of others?	_____	_____	_____
Needy, believing you cannot take care of yourself?	_____	_____	_____
Unsatisfied, unfulfilled, no matter what you do?	_____	_____	_____
Stingy, afraid you will not have enough?	_____	_____	_____
Paranoid, like you can't trust the world?	_____	_____	_____
Financially in trouble?	_____	_____	_____
Preoccupied with food, money, control?	_____	_____	_____
Unworthy, undeserving?	_____	_____	_____

If you answered yes to any one of these questions, your foundation is somewhat imbalanced. If you answered yes to two or three questions, you are slightly imbalanced and should follow the suggestions for adjusting slight imbalances at the end of this chapter. If you answered yes to four to eight questions, your foundation is moderately imbalanced and you should follow the suggestions for adjusting moderate imbalances. If you answered yes to nine or more questions, your foundation is seriously weakened and you should follow the suggestions for serious imbalances in order to help you heal.

HOW DID I LOSE MY BALANCE?

Many things can upset the balance of your first chakra; some are rooted in the past, and some are in the present. From the past, by far the most influential element is the family environment you encountered at your birth and during your early years. If you grew up in a loving and stable environment, one in which your parents and caretakers were generous and reliable, giving you what you needed easily and effortlessly, chances are you have a very solid and grounded foundation. Unfortunately, many of us were not born into such ideal conditions. More common are stressful, even chaotic homes, where one or both parents was challenged or ineffective, for whatever reason, in taking care of you, destabilizing your natural psychic equilibrium. Conditions such as not having enough money, attention, space, affection, community, or comfort when growing up can weaken our foundation. So can being exposed to threatening or untrustworthy people, such as people who are chronically angry or unreliable. Another unsettling influence is being uprooted from familiar surroundings without preparation or warning, such as moving into a new home, new school, or new social circle. Even frequent travel can destabilize our foundation, as can venturing into the unknown, particularly when we are very young.

As for the present, conditions that can unsettle your foundation include changing jobs, losing a job, not having a job or reliable means of support, or working in a job you do not like or where you feel others are not on your team. Getting married, getting divorced, ending a relationship, fighting and arguing, having a baby, getting into an accident, becoming ill, having an affair, or entering a new relationship, especially where you feel vulnerable, can throw your foundation out of balance. So can experiencing the sudden illness or death of someone you love, or getting a new boss. Taking care of someone who is sick or handicapped or suddenly dependent upon you can destabilize your foundation. In other words, the first chakra can be imbalanced by any condition that threatens your sense of stability, familiarity, predictability, security, or safety. Life itself can be very destabilizing. All unexpected or unpleasant events, the "psychic earthquakes of life," can challenge our foundation and throw us off balance. The worst upsets, however, are not the things that do happen. In fact, most people are extraordinarily adaptable to crises. The most unsettling element to our foundation is thinking and worrying about change before it happens. This unnerves us more than anything.

For example, my client Barbara originally called me urgently to request an appointment. She said she had visited an energy healer because she kept having minor accidents, usually the result of tripping over her own feet. None of her falls resulted in a serious injury, but they were nevertheless very unsettling. Her healer told her this was happening because she had a shaky foundation and was ungrounded. She had no idea what the woman meant and wanted me to help her understand it better. I explained to Barbara that when a person feels ungrounded, it is often because they are entering uncharted waters, and I asked her if she was facing any uncertainty in her life at this time. "Our first chakra is our connection to the Earth," I said, "and having a first chakra problem essentially means that you are in a period in your life where you aren't especially sure-footed. If you aren't sure where you are going or are not taking solid steps, the chances of you falling over go way up. Is that the case for you?"

Barbara laughed and asked, "This couldn't have anything to do with the fact that I am considering leaving my job of twenty years to venture out on my own, could it?"

"Of course it does," I said. "It has everything to do with it! In fact,

I'm sure this is exactly what is causing you to stumble. If you'll notice, a job is a source of support. It pays our bills, puts food on the table, brings us security. If you are changing that source, it destabilizes you, especially if you are moving from predictability to uncertainty. Hence, your energy field is reflecting your psychic condition, leaving you ungrounded and off balance. That explains why you may be accident prone. To remedy your problem, think about what you are doing, and don't force anything until you feel more certain."

"So," she said, "you believe I'm uncertain about changing careers, and that's why I keep falling down?" "Yes!" I said. "I do. Once you understand how your energy system works, and how it reacts to your mental state, even to the point of affecting your physical body, the problem becomes obvious. In order to regain your balance, you need to come to terms with your new path. It's not so much the urge to change that is destabilizing you as your waffling. It's as if you were waffling while changing lanes when you are driving. If you vacillate back and forth and don't commit to either one lane or the other, you not only throw yourself off, you throw everyone around you off as well. That's why you must be sure-footed. It can cause accidents if you aren't."

I went on. "At some point you must either make a decision and act on it, or forget about it until you feel ready. Just move out of limbo, Barbara. Then your foundation will rebalance, and you will be back on track." With that advice, Barbara decided to stay a little longer in her present job, until she had a better idea of what she wanted to do. Three short months later, she was offered an early retirement package as a part of a merger deal. With that healthy financial backup, she was able to let go of her job easily and painlessly. Now she is presently working part-time at a florist's shop and learning the art of flower arranging, something she has always wanted to do. And by the way, she hasn't tripped since.

VISITING THE PAST

How grounded was your family of origin?

_____

Did you feel safe and secure growing up?

_____

Was your family active in a church? Club? School?

_____

Did you move? Change schools? Neighborhoods? Towns? How often?

_____

Did your mother, father, or any other significant caretaker die when you were young?

_____

VISITING THE PRESENT

Have you recently:

Changed jobs?   Gotten married?   Divorced?   Moved?

Entered a new relationship?   Lost someone through death?

Gone back to school?   Lost a pet?

If you answered yes to any one of these questions, chances are you are somewhat ungrounded. If you answered yes to several of them, you may be in the middle of an energetic earthquake. Hang in there. Be kind to yourself, and refer to the suggestions at the end of the chapter for gaining your ground once again.

SOLID, NOT FIXED

Maintaining a balanced foundation is an ongoing and at times tricky process because it actually requires that you adapt to the ever-changing nature of life, bending like the branches of a tree to its ebb and flow while maintaining your roots. Though it is important to have stable and predictable conditions in your life when it comes to safety and security, it is neither reasonable nor realistic to insist that life be either stable or predictable in order to be secure. It isn't. Rather than trying to control your external environment, which none of us can ever do, it is far more reasonable and grounding to create an inner environment that supports you, which you can always do. Pay attention to what calms your spirit, soothes your soul, and helps you feel safe and secure in the world, and then to the best of your ability, regardless of the conditions around you, preserve those conditions, no matter what.

For example, though I love writing books and talking with people, I have discovered that going on lengthy speaking tours or working away from home for longer than a week at a time is very ungrounding, not only for me but for my family as well. After all, a family is a system, and when one person is off balance, it can't help but affect everyone else. Airports, hotel rooms, bad food, the effort of travel itself all wear me out and leave me feeling in need of the familiar and comfortable in a big way. My being gone also destabilizes my husband and children, who depend upon me to sustain the family dynamic that we've set up. It's not that I don't like to travel, because in fact I love it. But after a certain period of time, I begin to miss the daily routines that give me a sense of belonging to my home and family. I miss the delicious and healthy food that my husband prepares. I miss the family rituals over dinner and at bedtime that give all of us a sense of safe haven and solidity. I miss chatting with the neighbors and having dinners with friends. Though lecturing and teaching around the country are a terrific part of my life, I have come to discern when it's just enough and when it's too much. And I maintain that pace. That's how I preserve my foundation: by recognizing what I need to feel safe, sound, and solid and not giving these things up, no matter what distractions the outside world or even my own mind may present.

A musician friend of mine, Mark, has discovered some simple coping techniques for maintaining his foundation while traveling. These include bringing along mint tea bags, eating oatmeal for breakfast (not always easy to find), and walking at a very even and steady pace, no matter how rushed he is. The outcome is that he stays grounded.

The more aware of and faithful you are to the rituals and routines that help you feel rooted, the more adaptable you will be when life throws you a curveball and you are required to make changes in a hurry. No matter what goes on around you, you will be able to maintain your balance and stay solidly grounded in your energy.

MAINTAINING YOUR BALANCE

What are your favorite grounding routines?

_____

In the morning?

_____

In the evening?

_____

Before bedtime?

_____

TRY THIS!

Honor Your Feet

To really stabilize and harmonize your psychic and emotional energy, massage and care for your feet. Among lovers, it's a beautiful exchange of care. In antiquity, washing and oiling someone's feet was one of the highest forms of honor. Massage your feet by starting at the ball of your foot and working toward the heel, and then concentrate on your toes. As an added bonus, schedule a monthly pedicure. This goes for men as well as women!

SOLID FOOTING

While being grounded is primarily an energetic condition, your foundation is also greatly affected by your physical diet. An essential element to having a sound foundation is providing yourself with adequate nutrition. Eating poorly or eating food that has no life force seriously undermines your foundation. No matter what your mental attitude is, if you do not give your physical vehicle enough nutrients to live on, your energy will be greatly diminished, throwing you way out of balance. Poor eating includes filler food, such as fast food and prepackaged foods that are far removed from any vital source of nutrition. I do not recommend that you become a member of the food police, but I do recommend that you be responsible in what you choose to fuel your own body with. Not eating a healthy diet also sets up a vicious cycle. If your foundation is imbalanced, you will crave nutrients, even if you are not hungry, causing you to overeat. This creates the likelihood that you will be preoccupied with eating and dieting as you strive to feel psychically nurtured through physical means. This could very possibly set up an eating disorder. The entire diet industry preys on the belief that you cannot trust your own body to support you, nor trust anything you put in it to keep you strong and healthy. And in our country, where fifty-five percent of the population is overweight, this is something to look at.

My friend John told me of growing up in a household of nine children where money was tight and food was scarce. He lived on a steady diet of boxed macaroni and cheese, with very few fresh vegetables, and he often went to bed feeling empty, if not hungry. Even though there probably was always just enough food to go around, it wasn't food that nurtured him, and he constantly felt in need of more. This nutritionally deprived atmosphere left him ungrounded and chronically fearful that he might go hungry or, worse, actually die of starvation.

Consequently, even after he grew up and left home, John was preoccupied with getting enough to eat. He worried about the next meal, often even before he'd digested the last one. He'd buy groceries the minute he got paid. He clipped coupons from the newspaper to save money and obsessed over always having food in the refrigerator. He'd be the first in line at any buffet, loading his plate with everything in sight and eating way beyond his comfort zone, with no regard for nutrition or food value. He confused quantity with quality. In spite of the volume of food he ate, John made such poor food choices that he was still undernourished. He became severely overweight. Piling food on his plate was an attempt to comfort his shaky root chakra and shore up his weak foundation. Eventually, he acknowledged that he was in trouble. Obese, insecure, and very isolated, he joined Overeaters Anonymous, where he learned to eat in a balanced and sensible way. He also learned how to provide himself with the emotional conditions that reassured his anxieties. Thus he was able to calm his fears and support his body in a genuine way. With effort his childhood insecurities receded, and he began to feel grounded, which was a new experience for him. It was like getting out of "energy hell," he said. "For the first time in my life, I actually feel as though I can relax." The vicious cycle of bingeing, dieting, and feeling remorse gave way, and he is now standing on a far more grounded foundation.

If you consciously understand the needs of the first chakra, you can nurture your spirit with love, compassion, and practical support, with a balanced home, good food, and caring practices and friends. To stabilize your first chakra, begin by eating on schedule and with a degree of ritual. Avoid eating on the run, skipping meals, or failing to nourish yourself properly. Take the time to prepare your food in a loving way. Bless your food before you eat it, asking that it nurture you—body, mind, and soul. Let your inner self know that you value your body and that you intend to take good care of your needs so that you feel safe and solid in your body. If you are consistent, your body will come to believe you.

HOW SELF-NURTURING ARE YOU?

What do you usually eat for breakfast? Lunch? Dinner?

_____

Do you eat on the run?

_____

Do you overeat? Do you obsess over food?

_____

Do you prepare your food with care?

_____

How well do you nurture yourself?

_____

SAFETY IS BASIC TO FOUNDATION

One of the elements of a balanced foundation is physical and emotional safety. Psychic safety, the freedom to be you, is just as important as physical safety to the balance of the first chakra. For example, one woman revealed to me that she feels very safe in terms of material possessions.

She has a beautiful home and many luxuries. "But," she said, "I don't have the safety to speak my mind in my relationship with my husband. I could never really tell him how I feel. He is a very opinionated man with a short fuse, and he becomes verbally abusive whenever anyone disagrees with him. If I ever dare to contradict him or confront him about a situation, he starts yelling, which makes me terribly afraid. I know letting him bully me around like this isn't good for me because I always feel anxious around him no matter what. But still, he pays the bills and provides me a home, so I've learned it's just best to keep my mouth shut."

Many people suffer from psychically threatening conditions that destabilize our foundation, leaving them feeling unsafe. These conditions include abusive relationships and jobs that leave us feeling dispensable, vulnerable to downsizing. Such conditions are rampant in companies today and are causing foundation crises across the country. Clients of mine who have been forced to work in these conditions don't know what to do. They feel anxious, depressed, and threatened, and they often use alcohol, drugs, or other addictive substances in order to gain some sense of control in their lives. Needless to say, these measures don't work and usually lead to a downhill cycle, creating the very outcome that is feared, which is losing their job and their support.

Again, it's not possible to control what goes on around you, but you can control what goes on inside of you. No situation really has power over you unless you give it that power. Even if you are in psychically ungrounding conditions, you can still remind yourself that it is nevertheless your choice to remain there (if you are staying), and that you are the one who ultimately creates your own sense of safety with your choices. If you suffer from threatening conditions, you can always look for alternatives that provide you with a basic sense of respect, appreciation, and security. Remaining in circumstances that leave you feeling threatened is very destructive for the first chakra. It is never necessary to live like a prisoner unless you are one, and even then no one can imprison your mind or spirit unless you allow it. Once you decide that you have a basic right to safety and choose it for yourself, the Universe will lead you to higher ground. But it won't drag you there, kicking and screaming all the way.

DO YOU FEEL SAFE:

In your home?

_____

With the people you live with?

_____

Where you work?

_____

If not, will you ever consider leaving?

_____

TRY THIS!

Keep Living Things in Your Home

One of the loveliest ways to begin to create a sound foundation is to introduce live things into your home. These can be birds and fish, cats and dogs, and other small animals, as well as plants. Live things create a welcoming and joyous environment to come home to. They can brighten even the bleakest day. In addition, the routines required to keep plants and animals alive and well have a grounding effect on you.

FOUNDATION AND RELATIONSHIPS

Another serious disruption to your foundation can come from cutting yourself off from your family, especially in a fit of anger or rage. Any self-righteous severing of family ties can severely imbalance your foundation or cause it to collapse completely. I've noticed that people who've run away from dysfunctional, alcoholic, or addiction-oriented families often have a very weak foundation. Although it seems reasonable and even desirable to cut yourself off from the people who have hurt you, doing so in a fit of anger never succeeds in restoring balance and achieving relief. The fact is that we do need to come to some sense of acceptance about our families of origin in order to create our own foundation. It is undisputedly true that many people have been grossly mistreated by their families, and they have suffered for it. Yet rather than severing all ties to the family, the better solution is to seek psychological and spiritual counseling in order to arrive at a genuine and compassionate forgiveness. Then, if your family's behavior is toxic for you, you can detach in a loving and rational way. This is a hard assignment for those who have been seriously abused, which is all the more reason to seek the help of expert healers.

Healing injuries to our foundation requires us to realize and accept that we are lovable and worthy of love and have a right to have our needs met without any negative repercussions. Coming to this realization can be very challenging, but it can be done. The best way to get help is to seek a combination of therapies, including counseling, bodywork or massage, and spiritual guidance, including a spiritual practice. Healing your foundation may require the support of all sorts of coaches, such as dance therapists, energy workers, music therapists, massage therapists, priests, rabbis, and even medical doctors. Don't be afraid to approach all the qualified people you need to give you the energy to heal.

My favorite healing programs include the Hoffman Process, an eight-day workshop for healing the wounds of childhood; the Hendricks Foundation Training, a three-day workshop on creating relationships; the Avatar Course, a workshop in learning the mechanics of creating; and A Course in Miracles, a study in the unbelievably powerful forces of forgiveness and love. All of these therapies will teach you to be your own parent, to love the inner child that's crying inside of you, and to take charge of your own safety and support, with the help of the Universe. These methods teach you to demonstrate physically that you are present and aware, and that you will take care of your needs lovingly, so that your inner child can join in the celebration of life.

LOOKING AT YOUR RELATIONSHIPS

Describe your relationship with your family of origin.

_____

_____

_____

Describe your relationships with friends.

_____

_____

_____

Describe your relationships in general.

_____

_____

_____

Describe your relationship with yourself.

_____

_____

_____

FAILED ATTEMPTS AT BALANCING

Because we are creative beings, we are forever attempting to balance our energy centers, even if we do not realize that this is what we are doing. But because we do not fully understand the cause of our distress, nor how to regain our balance, our attempts often fail, leaving us more frustrated than before. For example, when I first moved to Chicago, I felt extremely ungrounded and insecure. As a way of trying to feel at home, I got the bright idea to go shopping for clothes that made me look more like a "chic Chicagoan" than like the hick from Denver that I felt I was. Week after week I would spend full paychecks at the local Ann Taylor store in a desperate attempt to blend in! Needless to say, it didn't work. In fact, it only made me feel worse. Although I looked good, I was both insecure and broke.

Over the years, I have noticed that I am not the only person who has attempted to get grounded that way. Hundreds of people with shaky foundations have spent fortunes on material possessions, hoping that these would settle their ungrounded feelings. Madison Avenue realizes this as well. The entire advertising industry preys upon a person's shaky foundation by promising that you will have more confidence, security, affection, and power if only you buy a certain product. If you've rowed that boat, as I have, I'm sure that you've already discovered that it doesn't work, although offering yourself a caring gift from time to time does. Just know what drives the purchase. Is it a loving gesture of appreciation toward yourself or a desperate attempt to buy security?

Another common way to try to strengthen our foundation is to conquer and control our physical bodies. In order to feel more secure, we strive for "buns of steel," "abs of iron," or some other unrealistic body image. I've been there, done that, too. My last attempt at getting grounded in a "body beautiful" fashion was to lift ten-pound weights more than two hundred times on day one of a great new exercise routine that was going to make me look the way I wanted to feel—better. I ended up with a strained shoulder. It took ten weeks to recover, and I felt more insecure than before because now I had to worry about reinjuring myself.

My younger sister also took a stroll down that dead-end road to security years ago, when she found herself in an unhealthy and unsafe relationship with a boyfriend who was forever criticizing her, especially about her appearance. Though she was five feet six inches and weighed only 110 pounds, he maliciously called her "fat," making her feel insecure and unnurtured. In an attempt to reassure herself and gain his approval, she bought vacuum pants that promised to "suck off her big hips," which she wore faithfully for weeks. They didn't work. According to him, she still had hips that wouldn't quit. Though she was attempting to regain her balance when wearing her vacuum pants, what she really needed was someone to wrap their arms around those hips and nurture her. She was trying to ground herself by altering her physical reality, when she actually needed to alter her emotional and energetic reality.

Eventually this guy went too far. In a lucid moment, she suddenly realized that what she really needed to vacuum out of her life was the lousy boyfriend, who was continually throwing her into doubt. She promptly did. The next man she met fell madly in love with her, and they married a few months later, to this day living happily ever after.

It sounds silly to try to ground yourself through such desperate measures, and yet who hasn't tried to do this at some time or other in their life? If the people I've met in my life, men and women alike, are any sampling of the norm, we are all guilty of these ridiculous behaviors. The truth is that these are attempts at seeking balance, and though sometimes they are seriously misguided, they are to be applauded. They demonstrate our innate desire to find the balance we so rightly deserve. We just need to do it in ways that bring better results.

What ridiculous thing have you done in the past to get more grounded?

_____

What ridiculous thing are you doing today to get more grounded?

_____

A SAFE HAVEN

Another essential element in having a balanced foundation is having a secure home. If your home gives you a sense of security and protection, then your first chakra will probably hum like a wheel, and you will feel as though you have a strong foundation. But if you live in tight quarters or in a space that doesn't give you a welcoming feeling, or if you end up suddenly moving into unfamiliar surroundings, don't be surprised if your foundation shows signs of strain and tips out of balance. If this occurs, you can even feel physical strain, which I experienced earlier in my life.

When I was twenty years old, I applied for a job with an airline on a whim. To my surprise, they hired me on the spot and told me I had to move to Chicago in two weeks if I wanted the job. I was thrilled at the chance and accepted the job, but as I prepared to move, I suddenly developed a mysterious pain that ran from my lower back down my leg. This pain was so severe at times that I could hardly walk. At some moments, I was completely paralyzed. Doctors diagnosed my problem as severe sciatica. My intuition diagnosed it as a shattered foundation due to the trauma of having to make such a major move on such short notice. Even though I really wanted to be on my own and see the world, I was still scared by all the sudden changes I was undergoing. Numerous visits from my parents and frequent trips home, finding an apartment with roommates whom I loved, and making regular visits to a sympathetic chiropractor cured my condition, but it took a while. As I developed new roots in Chicago and created a new sense of home, the pain eased. Ever since that episode, I have had a deep respect for the importance of having a secure sense of home in creating a solid foundation.

Over the years, I've met many people who have also developed leg and back disorders when their security or foundation was disrupted or when they faced a challenging condition such as the loss of a job, home, marriage, money, a pet, even their youth. Anytime we lose something that provides us with a sense of belonging or safety in the world, our foundation will be upset. It is therefore important to create the most comforting conditions to live in, both emotionally and aesthetically. I realize that finances can determine this to some degree, but even so, imagination can compensate where money falls short. Scouring the resale ads, for example, or shopping in discount shops can yield some excellent buys that will enhance any home.

Use your creativity to invent an atmosphere that, as my mother says, "is truly worthy of you." Don't settle for conditions that are depressing. If you can choose to, live only with people who calm your spirit. I do realize that when I say this, half of the married population of this country will say, "Then I guess I must divorce," because as we all know, no one pushes our buttons faster than our spouse. But establish to the best of your ability the most harmonious conditions you can. I believe you should leave no stone unturned in creating a safe haven for yourself, and this includes your most intimate relationships. If you have problems, flush them out and work on them. Don't settle for living in fear. You deserve better. You set the standard for your safety, and my advice is to set it very high.

HOME SWEET HOME

Is your home:

Attractive?   Pleasant?   Comfortable?   Clean?   Calming?

Welcoming?   Quiet?   Peaceful?   Safe to live in?

Can you think of any way to improve the energy in your home? How?

_____

_____

_____

_____

 TRY THIS!

Salt Your Home

Rituals speak directly to the subconscious mind. Here's an ancient one for grounding a home that I learned from my Eastern European friends. When they want to clear away negativity, they simply throw a little salt throughout the house, at every entrance, at every window, in all the corners and closets. When you do this, you needn't be excessive. A little pinch will do the trick. This ritual may seem a bit bizarre, but if you try it, you may be surprised at how effective it is. Salt properties are grounding. Don't we use the expression "salt of the earth" to mean someone solid?

ORDER FOR GROUNDING

Order is also necessary for a balanced foundation. Chaos creates stress on your energetic body, and if you allow yourself to live in chaos, it will be nearly impossible to feel grounded. Order offers a sense of certainty and predictability. Establishing order eliminates distractions so you stay connected to what is beneficial to you. The more order you live in, the more grounded you will be. Examine your life, and notice how orderly and organized it is. If necessary, create order for yourself as quickly as possible. If you cannot create order in your entire home, at least find a spot for yourself and create order there. You need enough organization in your home to give you a sense of relief and comfort when you walk through the door.

Order will also help you see the patterns in your life, so you know what you can count on and what you need to change. Creating a sense of security is a spiritual act that does not depend on external circumstances. It is a belief you carry within you that life is fine and you are safe. If you have security, you are free to seek productive and creative ways of living. You are also able to do more of the things you like and enjoy. Order is at the foundation of this kind of security. Order, in fact, is the foundation of foundation.

ASK YOURSELF:

Is your life in order?

_____

Are you organized?

_____

Can you add more order to your life? How?

_____

_____

TAKING RESPONSIBILITY

Another basic requirement for a grounded foundation is to stop waiting for someone else to give you what you need and instead to give it to yourself. Until you do this, you will not feel secure, even if all your material needs are met.

Let me tell you a story about a man named Marty who married Joanne, a successful screenwriter. Joanne provided the energy and the money to their marriage, while Marty spent his time philosophizing about life, uncertain and unwilling to commit to any creative interests of his own. This was fine with Joanne because she was happy doing work she loved, and she liked having Marty available to her. Surprised by her own prosperity, she invited her husband to fully share in her successes; she didn't care whether he worked or not. She didn't understand that her overly generous nature actually crippled his ability to build his own foundation.

Although he lived a comfortable life free of financial demands, Marty never felt secure or happy. He couldn't take a seat at the banquet that Joanne had set because he felt as though he didn't deserve to be there, having nothing to contribute himself. To cover up his insecurities, he constantly criticized her and the life they shared. At first she tried to cheer him up, trying to convince him to take a chance on his own creative pursuits, but he wouldn't. Finally, he wore her down, and one day, after yet another miserable disagreement, she said, "You know what? You're right. Since you won't roll up your sleeves and contribute, and you can't enjoy life with me, maybe you and I should separate." And they did! Rightfully so, as far as I was concerned.

Until Marty took responsibility for meeting his own needs, he was insecure: losing Joanne would mean losing his security as well, which was an awful feeling to live with. Meanwhile Joanne, who was paying all his bills while being resented for it, also failed to feel supported or secure. Since their separation, they have both found greater personal balance, Marty in paying his own bills, and Joanne in not using her money to buy companionship.

As this story demonstrates, you will not feel energetically grounded if you are riding on someone else's coattails instead of creating your own genuine support system. When it comes to your foundation, unless it is *your* foundation, you won't feel secure. No one can balance you but you. Ask yourself: "What am I doing to support myself? What am I contributing that I feel good about?" It doesn't necessarily have to be money, but it does have to reflect your efforts and talents.

A balanced foundation comes with the desire to grow up, show up, and take your place in life. It says, "I need certain things in order to live, and I'm going to get them through my own efforts." It says, "I can be counted on." A balanced foundation asks that you assume responsibility for your part and be willing to do whatever it takes to create the kind of security you desire. One of the cornerstones of a grounded foundation is thus the development of our talents. Any talent needs time and patience to grow. Time is associated with the first chakra, because, just like the seeds that are planted in a garden, balance cannot bloom to its full potential without a certain passage of time. Our talents, too, begin as seedlings of potential, and unless we nurture them over a period of time, they will not be able to support us. Patience is required for all things connected with our earthly existence.

So take a look at your work ethic and ask yourself if you are digging in. Are you committed to assuming full responsibility for your survival? If you are, you are well on your way to a solid foundation.

How responsible are you?

_____

Do you take responsibility for yourself?

_____

Can you pay your own bills? Do you?

_____

Describe your work habits. Would others describe you as reliable?

_____

Are you secretly waiting for someone else to assume financial responsibility for you?

_____

Do you keep your agreements and honor your commitments?

_____

If there was no one else around to take care of you, could you take care of yourself? Financially? Emotionally?

_____

HONESTY IS OUR FOUNDATION

One habit that undermines a solid foundation is to take what we have no right to take. For example, I've known petty thieves who steal office stationery or cheat on their hours by taking inordinately long lunches. Others steal by having a bad attitude, avoiding responsibilities with excuses and blaming, or looking busy when they are really not doing anything at all. In our maturation process, I believe we all go through phases where we try to see what we can get away with. As we move into adulthood, it's normal to go through this kind of testing. It's when you persist in avoiding responsibility, or continue to take what you haven't really earned, whether or not anyone notices, that you are seriously compromising your foundation. Even though you may justify your behavior, the truth is it's dishonest. And when you are dishonest, you do not have a solid foundation. It's that simple. I've been guilty of this kind of dishonesty in my own life.

When I was in my early twenties, for example, I moved to France to study in school. While I was there, I lived with different families who took very good care of me. For the most part, my day-to-day existence was quite comfortable. Nevertheless, whenever my parents or brothers and sisters called me, I would sing the "blues," telling them my life there was difficult and expensive and that I was really struggling. To some degree, this was true. Life was emotionally difficult, and I was frustrated because I had little spending money. But to paint my life as bleak as I did was definitely an exaggeration. Sympathetic, my family would send me money, believing they were keeping me from starvation, when in fact they were giving me shopping money. It took only a few of these donations before I began to feel like a creep. Every check I received undermined my self-esteem, because I had presented myself as weak and needy when I knew in my heart that it wasn't true. I wasn't weak and needy—I was ungrounded and broke, and I wanted to shop in Paris.

Though the sums of money were small, I finally decided that the price I was paying for being manipulative just wasn't worth it. I stopped whining for donations and got a job as a translator instead. This turned out to be the best experience I had in Paris. Assuming full responsibility for myself, I even managed to pay my family back. Taking this kind of moral inventory is very stabilizing to a shaky foundation. When you are so honest that you can be scrutinized by anyone at any time and come out clean, you can be certain that you are solid and safe in the world. It is a terrific feeling.

If you are tempted to cheat—and frankly almost every human being is at some time or other—stop and examine how you feel when you do cheat, even if no one is ever the wiser for it. Don't be surprised if you feel weak, lousy, and unsteady. In most cases, cheating arises from arrested development, or it's a bad habit, and with a little attention to just how costly these digressions are to your foundation, you will naturally resist the temptation to engage in it. If cheating is a problem, however, you should consider getting some help. Go to a therapist, a clergyman, or a self-help group like a twelve-step group for counsel. Cheating is not worth living with. The ground you'll gain by being honest will be more valuable than anything you could ever get out of cheating.

The corollary to cheating is being unduly suspicious of others, and this is another symptom of an imbalanced foundation. Feeling that there is not enough to go around leads you to constantly suspect others, fearing that they may take what is yours. Miserliness is a version of this affliction, where we give little effort and want maximum return. This can be manifested in attitudes like "I don't want to work hard" or "It's not my fault" or "I want something for nothing." Even though these impulses sound terrible, the truth is that sometimes we are all guilty of them. It may have been the time you asked a doctor at a party to prescribe medicine or diagnose your condition, hoping to get a free consultation. Or maybe you couldn't resist asking the attorney who lives next door to help you out of your lease, or maybe you bummed a ride to work while conveniently forgetting to offer gas money. These are all symptoms of a weak or imbalanced foundation because they demonstrate an unwillingness to take responsibility for something that we need.

None of these digressions are terrible in and of themselves, but they are damaging when practiced on a regular basis. And besides, we are only kidding ourselves if we believe our behavior is not transparent.

People are not that easily fooled. A manipulator or a deadbeat can be spotted a mile away, although people are often too polite to confront them directly. If you are guilty of these qualities, rest assured that people will talk about you, which is terrible for anyone's sense of energy and safety in the world. So if you have a tendency to take more than you give or to begrudge people their worth or to suspect everyone of cheating, wake up to it. Resolve to assume full responsibility for whatever you need in life, and give up taking advantage of others. Work out exchanges with those who can help you when you need it, and be willing to offer your best in return. A balanced foundation is built upon a sense of honesty. It ensures that the give and take of life is in harmony. It ensures that you are reliable and safe to be around. Nothing is more satisfying in life than knowing you can count on yourself in such a way. Nothing should keep you from enjoying that kind of unshakable security. And only you can choose it for yourself.

SCRUTINIZING YOURSELF

Do you cheat when you can get away with it? (Be honest.)

_____

In what areas of life are you tempted to cheat most?

_____

Do you tell white lies? Manipulate? Take more than is fair? Get others to do your work? If so, in what areas of your life?

_____

How do you feel about these digressions?

_____

If you recognize signs of an imbalanced foundation in yourself, take heart. We all have episodes of imbalance, especially when it comes to our foundation. The reason is that growth itself can be imbalancing. The point is that we must learn to recognize imbalances as they arise and correct them along the way, day by day, even moment to moment.

You can awaken and balance your first chakra in many different ways. Since the first chakra governs support, you can begin to nurture it by nurturing that which supports you, starting with your own physical body and then moving into your spirit. You can balance the first chakra by soothing your skin, working on your feet, strengthening your legs, properly feeding your body, comforting your emotions, and reassuring your soul. Creating order, gaining support, and being honest and ethical in all the workings of your life can strengthen it.

Foundation is laid by assuming a hundred percent responsibility for yourself and not waiting for others to take care of you. If your introduction to life wasn't loving and supportive, you can choose to correct this and begin to lay your own foundation today. Decide to move beyond the fact that you didn't get enough from your original caretakers, and for heaven's sake, stop treating yourself in the same unloving manner. Choose to give yourself the nurturing you need in life. Hand yourself the spoon, the plate, and the fork. Provide yourself with what you require in order to be fully grounded and present in life. Doing so will heal your foundation of old cracks and injuries and will help balance you this very moment, thus allowing you to fully experience your right to receive support as a child of the Universe.

RESTORING FOUNDATION

When you are *slightly* imbalanced

- Organize your drawers.

- Thoroughly clean your house.

- Sleep with a hot-water bottle.

- Wear good socks.

- Wear well-made, solid shoes.

- Take off your shoes when entering your home.

- Buy the best quality facial and bath tissue you can afford.

- Take a kick-boxing or aerobic dance class, or rent a kick-boxing or aerobic dance video and follow along.

- Carry a bloodstone (found at a local rock shop) in your pocket, and hold it when you feel shaky.

- Rub Vicks VapoRub on your feet, and then put on warm socks.

- Lie on the ground or roll down a hill.

- Go to bed earlier.

- Eat one balanced, home-cooked meal a day.

- Wear something red (the color of the first chakra).

When you are *moderately* imbalanced

- Cook your own meals; baking bread and peeling potatoes are especially grounding.

- Rent the movie *Matilda* by Danny DeVito.

- Listen to your body, and honor its signals.

- Work in the garden.

- Spend the weekend quietly at home.

- Set the breakfast table for yourself before bed.

- Make an appointment with a nutritionist, and improve your diet.

- Go for a long, leisurely walk in nature at least once a week.

- Take a short, brisk walk near your home every day.

- Have a picnic.

- Pay your bills on time.

- Tell the truth.

- Honor your agreements and commitments.

- Straighten up your desk.

- Eat beets, turnips, potatoes, carrots, and other root vegetables.

When you have a *major* imbalance

- Join a support group such as AA, Al-Anon, or ManKind Project (a men's mentoring group; see Resources).

- Get regular massages with a certified massage therapist for two to three months, or go to the local massage therapy training school and volunteer for free massages by one of the students.

- Take a workshop in self-love and self-care, such as Hendricks Foundation Training, the Avatar Process, or the Hoffman Process.

- See a therapist on a regular basis.

- Join an inspiring church.

- Take a class on healthy cooking.

- Get a pet.

- Make amends to those you've cheated.

- Make peace with your family of origin.

- Take a gardening course.

- Get to know your neighbors.

- Spend time with your family.

- Establish comforting routines.

Remember, foundation is

Security
Safety
Work
Order
Routine
Nurturance
Nutrition
Fairness
Organization
Honesty
Flexibility
Responsibility
Health

As you regain balance in your foundation, your spirit will inspire your own personal ways for maintaining this balance. Write down all your remedies for balance in the space below:

_____

_____

_____

_____

OUR EMOTIONAL AND SENSUAL well-being, our vitality, resides in the second chakra. This energy center, located in the lower abdomen, beckons our spirit into the earthly experience through emotion, desire, sexuality, sensuality, feeling, and pleasure. It activates all of our senses, including sight, sound, taste, touch, and smell, as well as our intuitive and emotional feelings. On a physiological level, this chakra channels life force into the sexual and reproductive organs, the bladder, and part of the lower intestine. If your second chakra is out of balance, you may experience difficulty with these parts of your body. On the color spectrum, the second chakra vibrates energetically to the color orange.

Activated shortly after birth as energy moves up from our foundation, this center of consciousness entices us to experience the joy of being alive. It awakens our appetites for life, whether for physical gratification or for emotional fulfillment. It drives our desires as well as our creative expression. Its mission statement is "I feel. I sense. I discover." It delights in our physical and emotional experiences and encourages us to partake of

Second Chakra

Balanced Vitality

the good life. It boosts our awareness of and desire for pleasure in every form. It is our internal feedback system for all that we encounter in life. Once our foundation is established, we travel into this second center of awareness and begin to explore what being human is all about. This energy center is the laboratory of personal discovery. It allows us to discover who we are and what life itself is through the world of feeling. Only through this center of consciousness can we directly participate in the world.

Our vitality center establishes in us a healthy enthusiasm for being alive. The Universe wants us to experience and enjoy life on Earth, not simply endure it or overcome it, as some spiritual practices would suggest. The physical world is an incredible playground for the human spirit, and it is through this energy station that we discover and express our Divine nature. Through this sublime center, we are able to drink from the cup of plenty and enjoy all that the Universe has to offer and wants to bestow upon us. It is the center of abundance, generosity, prosperity, and flow.

FEELING GOOD IN YOUR SKIN

One of my favorite French expressions is *"Je me sens bien dans ma peau,"* which means literally "I feel good in my skin." This expression summarizes better than any other what the second chakra is all about. This marvelous sensation center, when balanced, creates passion for life. Being governed by physical sensation, it celebrates gatherings, connections, and togetherness with others, good food, good wine, good song, good sex, and good times. It expresses humor, candor, mirth, and spontaneity. It moves us to join with others in the celebration of life. It awakens our graciousness and affection. One of its greatest hallmarks is romance, the gateway to the heart, and through the sensual zone, we are seduced into learning to love.

I like to imagine the vitality center as a fireplace in the belly, warm, exciting, and inviting. It awakens the flavor, color, richness, and depth of our souls. It is the center of our human passion, and if this fire is kept burning, we are capable of unbelievable accomplishments. All that brings beauty, intensity, and life force to our world arises out of this center. It is where we first feel the incredible potential of our Divine nature to express and create. It releases our wild side and instills in us a freedom to express ourselves in the most elemental, honest, and self-aware way. From this center, the infant laughs with abandon when pleased and screams with fury when angered. It allows our feelings free rein and expression without censorship, editorializing, or restraint, and it accepts all that we feel as part of our natural Divine makeup.

DESIRE AND INGENUITY

Our second chakra, our feeling center, activates inspiration and ingenuity. Propelled by desire, it stimulates our ability to create the kind of experiences we want. This energy sets itself free in all of us at an early age. Left uncensored, our feeling center ignites our resourcefulness and urges us to find creative ways to manifest what we really want. Its primary impulse is to gratify our desire, and it will push us into finding every possible way to do so. It is the engine of invention.

Let me tell you a story about my five-year-old niece, Noelle, and the inventive power of her vital chakra. When she was in kindergarten, she suddenly had an intense desire to own a pair of silver shoes. It was springtime, and as much as her mother wanted to fulfill her desire, she explained to Noelle that silver shoes were more Christmastime shoes; the only ones she could find at that time were either white or yellow. But Noelle, wanting silver shoes more than life itself, insisted that my sister take her to the mall to look anyway. Together they searched from store to store, with no success. Finally, they had to give up. Having given it her best shot as a supportive parent, my sister was sure that she had finally convinced Noelle to let go of her whim. My sister, who was a flight attendant, went on a flight the next morning.

When she returned two days later, her husband, Bud, said, "You've got to go into Noelle's bedroom and see what she created." There, in the corner of the little girl's room, sat a pair of silver shoes! Noelle, not to be deterred from fulfilling her desire, had covered her black patent-leather shoes inside and out with aluminum foil and then completely covered the foil with Scotch tape. Seeing her mom admiring her handiwork, Noelle came up behind her and said proudly, "Don't you love my shoes? I wore them to school, Mom, and everybody liked them as much as I do." This is the power of desire in action.

HOW INVENTIVE ARE YOU?

What have you created in your life that has brought you pleasure? (This could be a home, a relationship, an adventure, art, and even a job that you like.)

_____

_____

What are you pursuing in your life now that brings you pleasure and satisfaction?

_____

_____

Are you able to give yourself the time and opportunity to create the things and experiences you really want?

_____

_____

List the things you would love to create in your life.

_____

_____

Do you have enthusiasm and passion for these desires?

_____

If not, what is in the way?

_____

THE GOOD LIFE

Balanced vitality inspires in you a sense of entitlement to the good things in life, whether they are good food and good friends, abundance and prosperity, comfort and pleasure, or simply being alive. This energy center activates your ability to make your own life a wonderful event. It awakens your royal nature and stimulates your imagination. It serves you the enticing bonbons, tidbits, and delicious extravagances of life. It's the seat of discovery, curiosity, and play. It's indulgence, richness, and sweetness; it's the bountiful garden bursting with flowers and fruits.

You can always tell a person who has balanced vitality by their wonderful sense of style and occasion. They are the ones who take the ordinary mundane routines in life and, with a splash of inventiveness, make them extraordinary. These are the people who garnish the plate before serving dinner, place fresh flowers by your bedside before kissing you good night, and decorate for the holidays. They are the ones who give beautifully wrapped gifts for no special reason and remember to call you on your anniversary or birthday when even you yourself forgot it was a special day. They get out the best china and silver for dinner and dress to go out to lunch. They are the preservers of tradition and mark the passing of time with flair, never losing touch with the wonder and wit of the world and constantly ushering in beauty. He or she may be your favorite uncle, your eccentric next-door neighbor, or your Old World grandmother. He or she may be you.

What are your favorite pleasures in life?

_____

How do you fulfill your passions?

_____

How would you spend a sensual evening with a friend or lover?

_____

What are some of your favorite extravagances?

_____

How do you preserve tradition?

_____

How do you celebrate occasion?

_____

TRY THIS!

Give Yourself Flowers

Treat yourself to fresh flowers on a regular basis. You can do this every week even when on a budget if you pay attention to the local specials at the florist shop and buy flowers that last a long time. Carnations, birds-of-paradise, and ginger, for example, last for well over a week in most cases and bring such beauty to your surroundings while costing only a few dollars. Even better are flowers with strong scents, such as tuberoses, roses, and lilies. Though they may seem like an extravagance, flowers feed the soul and nurture a person in such a deep way that they are well worth the expense.

IMBALANCED VITALITY

If your second chakra, your vitality center, becomes imbalanced, you may avoid, control, or ignore your feelings or—even worse—disconnect from your sensuality altogether, so that you are "living in your head." When this center is out of balance, you lose touch with or ignore what your body tells you, neglecting to take care of it, pushing beyond its limits and refusing to nurture or be kind to it in any way. Often, if the imbalance is great enough, you can even get to the point where self-denial, self-rejection, and self-deprivation overshadow your life. You can lose all spontaneity, pleasure, and joy whatsoever. Even a small act of deprivation—never allowing yourself dessert after dinner, not allowing yourself to buy a beautiful piece of clothing or art for your home, or always taking a strictly utilitarian approach to life—can be a sign of an imbalanced second chakra. This is not to say that you must indulge every whim and fancy, because that too is imbalanced. But when you have a difficult time accepting any sweetness in life, your second chakra is definitely leaning on tilt. People who lived through the Great Depression, for example, often had an imbalanced second chakra because during those years sensual experiences were ignored due to the overwhelming need to focus on survival. Even though the Depression has come and gone, many people were so impacted by that scourge of deprivation that they never really got over it, continuing to live as if there were so little to go around that they must deny their urges for any indulgences. My father, for example, is a very generous man, but he still has a strong tendency to deny himself; he is always quick to argue that he "doesn't need a thing." Perhaps you know someone who has a tendency to do this as well. It wouldn't be surprising because so many of us have been raised in environments where our needs were met but our desires weren't, so we continue to ignore our desires as well. Our vitality, our sensual nature, however, isn't about need. It's about generosity and flow. When we have a difficult time receiving, we block the flow of life.

More pernicious and disabling symptoms of imbalanced vitality are anorexia, bulimia, addiction, sexual dysfunction, and depression. All of these conditions reflect to some degree an attempt to repress or control our sensual nature, throwing our emotional and physical systems into chaos and darkness. When we reject, repress, deny, or ignore any of our feelings or sensations for an extended period of time, we enter into a state of dysfunction that is no less disabling to us than if we were to reject our hands or our feet. When we block our feelings, our ability to have a complete and satisfying human experience is crippled, because we deny ourselves the gifts of life.

TRY THIS!

Create Your Own Spa

Create your own day spa by taking off a morning or afternoon with no agenda other than to nurture yourself completely. Start by giving yourself a facial. Mud or seaweed facial packs are available over the counter at most cosmetic or health food stores for a couple of dollars. Mix one up, slather it on, and then soak in a warm tub filled with two or three cups of mineral salts (also available at most health food stores) for at least an hour while listening to your favorite classical CD. Follow up with a cool shower, and then apply warmed body lotion all over. Complete your experience by sipping a cup of hot cocoa topped with marshmallows or your favorite herbal tea and reading a few chapters from a delicious romance or adventure novel.

You can also experience the pampering effect of a spa without the cost by visiting a school of beauty or a school for massage therapy and volunteering to have the students practice on you. Usually you'll receive great care, as the students are extremely attentive to doing things right.

WAKING SLEEPING BEAUTY

I had a client named Crystal with long, flaming red hair that seemed to reflect her passionate sensuality. But paradoxically, even though Crystal's lovely hair promised a depth of feeling, the truth was that she was totally cut off from her sensual side. She had abandoned it early in life in response to her mother, who had run Crystal's young life with cold, austere detachment. In Crystal's house, feelings were not only unacknowledged but scorned. Only intellectual knowing was valued, and the family mantra was "Use your head." Not surprisingly, Crystal figured out that the best way to win approval in this environment was to shut off her feelings and focus her attention exclusively on her intellectual accomplishments. She went on to earn a Ph.D. in mathematics and the respect of her peers, but the rigorous study, the relentless pressure to perform, and her refusal to be good to herself ended by making her sick and deprived. By the time she came to see me, she had disowned her body, her femininity, and her sexuality. Chronically controlling her feelings and denying herself even the most basic pleasures in life, she had become anorexic as well.

Crystal's imbalance was so severe when I first met her that she was nearly dying of starvation. Her vitality definitely needed a jump start so that she could reconnect with her body and begin to heal. Although she knew she was in trouble, she didn't know how to help herself. As a start, I sent her to a wonderful massage therapist who could nurture her while teaching her how to appreciate her body. Much as Crystal enjoyed receiving these massages, she resisted the pleasure by talking nonstop and by distracting herself from being truly present. Finally the therapist asked her to remain silent and simply allow herself to feel her body each time they met. That was a whole new concept to Crystal and one that took some getting used to. In silence she felt far more vulnerable and restless. The therapist informed her that this was because she wasn't used to experiencing her feelings and encouraged her to stick with it in spite of the discomfort. At first Crystal was restless, then angry, then sad, and finally filled with compassion for herself. Each massage unleashed a new wave of unfelt feeling that had been pent up for years.

After six months of intense and regular massage therapy, Crystal began to soften in her body, trusting that it might actually be a place worth exploring. After six more months of therapy, her sensuality began to stir. She even began to feel sexy! Intrigued, she began to explore other sensual therapies like dance, drumming, aromatherapy, and art and makeup classes. Slowly and subtly her vitality came alive. Crystal described it as "moving from a world that was black and white and into one that was in color." Rather than ignoring that she had a body, draping it under drab and shapeless clothing, she started to celebrate her body. She began taking yoga. She dressed in beautiful clothing and got her hair and nails done. She began to feel as beautiful, sexual, and alive as she actually was. She also began to enjoy food—another miracle, given that she had battled with it for over twenty years. Her eating disorders eased up as she reconnected with her earthy self. She began preparing and sharing food with friends and family, not just to sustain herself, but to actually celebrate togetherness.

In reconnecting with her vitality, Crystal was ushered into a world that thoroughly delighted her. Life became a wonder. It was no longer the dreary and painful existence that she had been trained to avoid. It became joyful, intriguing, rich, and flavorful—and at times even lusty. It remains a challenge for Crystal to honor her body and sensuality, because old habits die hard. But she's motivated by all the fun she is having! She said to me the other day, "Isn't it amazing that I had to be taught to feel?"

CHECKING YOUR VITALITY

	Yes	No	Sometimes
Do you enjoy your body?	_____	_____	_____
Nurture your body?	_____	_____	_____
Listen to your body?	_____	_____	_____
Pay attention to your feelings?	_____	_____	_____
Express your feelings?	_____	_____	_____
Respect your feelings?	_____	_____	_____
Take the time to eat well and sleep enough?	_____	_____	_____
Treat yourself gently?	_____	_____	_____
Take the time to look nice?	_____	_____	_____

Enjoy wearing attractive clothing?	_____	_____	_____
Enjoy being sexual?	_____	_____	_____
Celebrate yourself and your accomplishments?	_____	_____	_____
Share good food and drink with friends and lovers?	_____	_____	_____
Mark the important occasions in life?	_____	_____	_____
Allow yourself little extravagances?	_____	_____	_____
Agree to receive and be nurtured?	_____	_____	_____
Create beauty in life?	_____	_____	_____

If you answered no to any one of these questions, your vitality is somewhat imbalanced. If you answered no to two or three questions, you are slightly imbalanced and should follow the suggestions for slight imbalances at the end of the chapter. If you answered no to four to seven questions, then you are moderately imbalanced and should follow the suggestions for adjusting moderate imbalances. If you answered no to eight or more questions, then your vitality is seriously weakened, and you should follow the suggestions for serious imbalances in order to help you heal and enjoy life more.

 TRY THIS!

Give Someone a Care Basket

One of the most nurturing things we can do for our own vitality is to nurture someone else's lagging second chakra. Surprise someone you love with a care basket filled with all sorts of sweet indulgences and nurturing goodies. For example, you might select a scented bath soap, an aromatherapy candle, some Belgian chocolates, a box of exotic herbal tea, an exotic essential oil, and even a sensual or sexy CD, such as jazz or something French. Let your own imagination run wild as you prepare this luxurious and romantic surprise.

VOLATILE EMOTIONS

Our vitality, being watery in nature, has a very changeable nature. Just as water will sometimes bring with it storms and waves, the emotions in life aren't always smooth. Often when unsettled feelings arise, people shut them down because they have been taught that unpleasant feelings are bad. In truth, feelings themselves are neither bad nor good but serve only to bring our focus to something that requires attention. Storms serve to clear the air, wash away the old, and bring life to the new. It's not our feelings themselves that cause us difficulty in life, but the repression or judgment of our feelings.

For example, a client named Bob was by all appearances the nicest, most even-tempered man you'd ever hope to meet. He was successful in business, was very good looking and in excellent health, and for all the world looked like a great guy. And yet for all the good things he had going for him, try as he might, Bob could not create a love life worth having. Because he felt so strongly that "being nice" and pleasant were the only acceptable emotions people should have, he had a hard time finding a partner who fit his requirements. Sometimes he dated nice, pleasant, low-key women. But they failed to hold his interest because of their lack of passion and intensity. Bored by their controlled veneer, he'd leave, looking for a little more excitement. And yet when Bob dated passionate women who expressed strong opinions and feelings like anger or resentment, their intensity would soon scare him, and he would run away, claiming they weren't "ladylike" or "nice" enough for him.

It was a vicious cycle of frustration. Bob craved the excitement and passion of the vital center, but he wanted to control this sensual flow at the same time. Try as I might to explain to him that the problem was more his fear of feeling any unpleasant feelings than his never meeting the right woman, he just couldn't see it that way. To him, it was simply a matter of finding the "perfect gal," one who in his mind would be polite, pleasant, ladylike, low-key, mothering, passionate, fiery, sexy, courageous, and wild. I tried to explain to him that it was highly unlikely that he would find these opposing characteristics in a real live human being, but he was convinced he would. His endless and futile search for passion without feeling still goes on. As crazy as it sounds, he has been engaged ten times in almost as many years, and minus a few diamond rings, he continues his quest.

Only in accepting the full spectrum of our senses and emotions do we come to fully embrace the human experience. Experiencing only the good would rob us of opportunities to grow, discover, and learn. Our darker, more difficult feelings are just as vital as our lighter, easier feelings. Feelings of all sorts, light and dark, are our teachers, alerting us to opportunities to grow in our understanding of ourselves, others, and the world we inhabit. Experiencing an unpleasant feeling may really be a gift. For example, the sting of a hot stove upon our fingertips teaches us that fire can burn us. This is good to know if we were planning on sitting on the stove! Pain is an inevitable part of the human experience, and we need to appreciate it for the messenger that it is. It becomes a problem only when we get stuck with the messenger and don't learn the message.

Feelings let us know when we have fallen out of harmony with our spirit. Unpleasant feelings let us know that we need comfort, sensual reassurance, and rebalancing. Sadly, many of us simply suffer through these blue episodes, waiting for some "prince" or "princess" to come along and give us what we need, which never happens. What we need to do during these blue periods is to accept responsibility for our feelings and begin to take care of ourselves.

I recently met a woman who was in the midst of a painful divorce from an abusive husband and at the same time was feeling very unappreciated in her job. These combined challenges left her depressed and imbalanced in her sensory center. She had a bad case of the "second chakra blues." One day, having had enough of feeling "not good enough," as she put it, she traded in her Dodge for a beautiful red sports car for no reason other than that she had always wanted one and was tired of waiting for someone else to give it to her.

Buying that car changed her entire perspective. Offering herself a beautiful gift, one that so genuinely appealed to her sexy side, was so empowering that she actually started feeling better. Shortly after her purchase, she had a sudden burst of confidence. She applied for a new job and was hired on the spot. Further empowered and feeling better all around, she overcame her natural reserve and actually began to smile and connect with the people she worked with. A few weeks into her new job, a coworker whom she had befriended offered to introduce her to her brother. The chemistry clicked. They began dating, and she discovered that she was having a great time for a change. "I could say that all it took was buying myself that car," she told me, "but I know it wasn't that. What really changed the way things were going was that one day I simply woke up and decided that I wasn't going to put my life on hold any longer, waiting for someone else to treat me better than I was willing to treat myself. The day I decided to be kind and appreciative of me, so did everyone else. The car was only symbolic. The real gift was my change in attitude."

WEATHERING THE STORM

Are you able to feel unpleasant feelings without repressing them or judging them as "bad"?

_____

How do you feel when you are exposed to someone else's unpleasant feelings?

_____

What do you do when you are in an emotional storm?

_____

Were the people in your family emotionally expressive?

_____

_____

Would you describe yourself as emotionally expressive or shut down?

_____

_____

Do you emotionally nurture yourself, or do you wait for someone else to do it?

_____

What is the last nurturing or indulgent thing that you did for yourself?

_____

_____

 ## TRY THIS!

Be Your Own Prince or Princess
Treat yourself to a long-desired special gift. It could be a beautiful watch, a down pillow, a great pair of shoes, or a night on the town. Set aside a few dollars every week for your special extravagance if you must, and have patience in case it takes a little time to save up. Don't let your rational mind talk you out of this special treat. A little sweetness goes a long way in nurturing your spirit and adding to your vitality, and you are well worth it!

TRY THIS!

Congratulate Yourself

The next time you do something well, whether it's giving a presentation at work or making lunch for your kids and their friends, stop and say out loud, "Wasn't I *great!*" Sing your praises without restraint. Reminisce about how well your success unfolded, replaying it scene by scene a couple of times. Don't hold back. Don't be stingy. Give yourself all the appreciation and enthusiasm that you have always secretly wanted to receive from others. Forget all modesty, and let the compliments fly.

TRY THIS!

When You Are Feeling Really Upset

The next time you feel overwhelmed with anger or frustration, don't "stuff your feelings." Let them out. To do so, pile a huge stack of pillows on your bed, and then, while imagining all that upsets you, beat the pillows wildly with your fists. As you let your fists fly, rant, rave, yell, and scream for all it's worth until you feel completely emptied of all pent-up emotion. The more you hold your feelings in, the better this remedy is for you. (Of course, it's best to try this particular suggestion when you're alone.)

ROMANTIC JUMP START

Whenever one of our seven energy centers is out of balance, we unconsciously move toward whatever we are missing, even if we are unaware that this is what we are doing. Pamela was a schoolteacher for disturbed children who lived in the Bronx with her parents. When she contacted me for a reading, she said, "Sonia, I really need some guidance. I think I must repel men. I have never had a date. I'm never asked out. I spend my evenings watching TV or gossiping with the neighbors, but never anything more exciting than that. I don't know what's wrong with me. Last summer I went to Rome and felt like it was a spiritual awakening. I have never been more inspired or alive in my life. I loved everything about it, the food, the art, the wine, and the pasta. While I was there, I met a very sexy man named Alessandro, who wined and dined me in royal fashion. I'm not sure whether I'm happy or embarrassed to admit it, but the day after we met, we made love, and it was wonderful. I feel as though he's my soul mate, and I can't get him off my mind. I would love nothing more than to be his wife, and I've been trying to contact him for months, but he won't return my calls. We were so close at the time, so I can't understand what's going on. I'm afraid to ask, but do you think he used me?"

After reflecting for a moment, I said, "No, Pam, as disappointed as you are about Alessandro's refusal to return your calls, I don't think you were used as you fear, even though I'm sure it feels that way. In fact, even though things didn't turn out the way you had hoped, I even think your experience with him was very healing." Confused, she asked, "What do you mean? In what way?" "Well," I continued, "before meeting Alessandro, your life was pretty much devoid of sensuality. You worked in a sterile environment, and though you are an adult woman, living with your parents cut you off from your own sensual and sexual nature. Your frustration level was very high, which is probably what compelled you to go to Rome in the first place. You were searching for balance, for what was missing in your life, your sensual nature.

"When you booked your ticket to Italy," I went on, "you booked a ticket into the land of romance, the domain of sensuality. It was the perfect place for you to go. Being there awakened your sensual nature, and thankfully so. Alessandro was simply part of that marvelous epiphany. He intuitively sensed that you were reclaiming your passionate nature and graciously helped you in your pursuit. Your experience with him was a positive one, and you felt it. And yet no matter how satisfying the time you spent together was, it is important to understand what the real gift was. What was so exciting was not so much Alessandro himself (although I can only imagine that he was as fabulous as you say) but rather the experience of awakening your own marvelous sensual and sexual nature. That is something intrinsic to you, and it does not depend upon Alessandro or any other man or situation to keep alive. As tempting as it is to give him all the credit, he was merely your muse. It is really the lost part of you that draws you in and that you want to remain in connection with. And you can. The way to do this, however, is not to chase Alessandro down and get married, which obviously is not an option anyway. You simply need to bring your sensuality home. Keep your passion, your desire, and your femininity alive, and enjoy it, in New York, in the moment."

Pam wasn't happy with my advice. She would have much preferred to hear that her prince would come and she would live blissfully ever after. But eventually she reported that, as painful as it was to hear, she knew in her heart that what I said was true. Motivated by the wonderful time she had had with Alessandro and how beautiful she felt afterward, she had a cosmetic makeover, fixed her teeth, and bought a new wardrobe. She also began to take Italian lessons, an Italian cooking class, and a course in *faux* wall painting, something she had always secretly wanted to do. Because her parents were dead set against *faux* anything in their home, she finally moved into her own apartment and set her creative urges free. The move also activated a love life. Several months into her newly awakened sensuality, she met Dennis, an Irish-American house-painter who was also looking for a little variety and spice in his life. He wasn't Italian, but he was passionate and adventurous. Last I heard, Pam and Dennis were planning a trip to Florence, and the passion was still running high.

YOUR SENSUAL SELF

Has your passionate nature been neglected?

_____

Do you depend upon someone else to make you feel sexy or sensual or bring excitement to your life?

_____

How are you presently expressing your own vitality, sensuality, sexuality, and passion? How are you bringing excitement into your life today?

_____

_____

TRY THIS!

Buy Sexy New Underwear

An excellent remedy for low vitality is to buy sexy new underwear. I mean underwear that not only makes you look sensual and sexy but also feels luxurious and wonderful on your skin. So no cheap stuff. The other half of this remedy is to throw away all of the old, ugly, worn-out, ratty underwear that you've kept and worn for way too long—the ones your mother warned you not to wear in case you had an accident and the paramedics arrived. This suggestion goes for men as well as women.

ROMANCE

One of the greatest expressions of our vitality is the intoxicating, all-encompassing luxury of a great romance. Unlike day-to-day life, romance freezes time and allows us to step out of our mundane existence and enter into the sublime territory of lovers from time immemorial. Romance is a gift, and whenever we find ourselves in it, it is like falling into a sweet dream.

Every day can be a romantic day. All it takes is an appreciation for the sweet and sensual beauty of life. Romance is less a matter of whom you meet than of who you are. All true romantics step off the treadmill of the mind and take time to smell (and give) the roses. My husband, Patrick, is my great teacher when it comes to romance. From the beginning of our relationship, he has always been inventive and sensual and romantic. He once invited me to ride my bicycle down to Navy Pier, along the lakefront in Chicago. When I did, he surprised me with a picnic basket of homemade sandwiches, fresh fruit, cookies, and chocolates, complete with a bud vase and a carnation. Never mind that it was raining cats and dogs. He had found an old barge where we could retreat from the rain, and there we sat, enjoying our repast high and dry. Patrick would write me poems and hide them under my pillow or in my sock drawer or coat pocket, to be discovered later, at a moment when I least expected it. He would paint me miniature watercolors, or sneak up and hug me when I wasn't looking. Until I met him, I fantasized about romance, but I never imagined that I myself could choose to be romantic. Patrick inspired me. Now I occasionally create the picnic, give the flowers, and write the love letters. And I can tell you that it is just as intoxicating to be the creator of romantic notions as it is to be on the receiving end.

Through Patrick I have learned that romance is a second chakra art form, and anyone who takes the time can become a member of the select group that understands this. All you need is the desire to feel pleasure and to bring pleasure to those you love. It isn't expensive, but it does require imagination. To awaken the romantic in you, awaken your senses. Ask yourself what soothes your soul. Let your senses direct you. What do you love to eat? To drink? What scents move your spirit? What colors ease your body? What music captures your heart? What works of art take you to other worlds? Romance is a sensory explosion. It is the world of sweet sound, taste, color, touch, flavor, and image. It is the world of soft focus and slow motion that reminds us to experience the moment in every way. It notices the subtle, the gentle, and the magic that abounds around us. It seduces us out of our mind-chatter and into the present, basking us in the delights of the human experience. It rescues us from the worries of life and gives us sanctuary. It is the perfect world of now, a place where all is Divinely right, and you are Divinely appreciated. To be a romantic, embrace beauty, and then share it with someone you love.

AWAKENING YOUR ROMANTIC SPIRIT

Describe your idea of a perfect romantic evening.

_____

_____

Describe the last romantic experience you had.

_____

Describe the most exciting romantic place you can think of.

_____

Have you ever received a love letter?

_____

Have you ever written a love letter?

_____

Describe the perfect lover.

_____

_____

Describe how you could be the perfect lover.

_____

_____

(Doesn't this sound fun?)

 TRY THIS!

Slow Dancing

Slow dancing is marvelous second chakra therapy. If you are lucky
enough to have a dancing partner, simply turn on the music, put a rose
in your teeth, and go for it. If, on the other hand, you are solo, enroll
in a class at a local dance school. Many cities have an adult learning
annex that charges as little as twenty dollars for a six-week course. If
you're hesitant and need a little inspiration, rent the movie *Shall We
Dance,* a Japanese film about a burned-out businessman who revives his
lagging vitality by secretly dancing after work. By the time the movie is
over, I guarantee you that your own feet will be itching to tango.

SENSUALITY VERSUS LOVE

We human beings are very resourceful in the ways in which we attempt
to bring relief to our imbalanced chakras, even though the remedies we
reach for are often ineffective. For example, a familiar but doomed belief
is that if a little of a good thing feels nice, then a lot of that good thing
must feel even better. Unfortunately, when it comes to our senses, this
rule doesn't apply. Instead of increasing our pleasure, excess leads to
addiction and leaves us frustrated, unfulfilled, and sick.

For example, a little chocolate is sweet, but too much makes us fat. A
little wine is soothing; too much makes us drunk. A little cheese and
bread are delicious, but too much gives us a stomachache. Many of us go
through addictive periods, often when we are facing the unknown and
need reassurance. This is because we have so little understanding of our
own nature that we confuse feelings of pleasure with feelings of love.
Both sensation and love deliver an initial surge of "feel good" energy.
But sensuality is very corporeal and temporary, changing from moment
to moment depending upon the external stimulation you are experiencing, whereas love is spiritual and consistent and completely independent
of any external, or physical, stimulation. Sensuality is basically a function of the body, while love is a function of the spirit. Failing to discern
the difference can lead to confusion, causing us to attach to sensation in

lieu of love. When this happens, we become frustrated, and because we can't sustain the high we crave, addictions kick in. The obsessive pursuit of any temporary pleasure will enslave us. We become driven by compulsion to control our feelings, wanting good feelings only as we attempt to escape from our fearful feelings. In the end, we are left numb.

If you have fallen into addictive patterns, you are attempting to nurture yourself in the wrong way. Most addictive behavior ceases only when we reach out to nurturing sources that can help ease our emptiness. Any twelve-step program is a godsend to people struggling with addiction. If you have an addiction problem, you must be suffering terribly. It isn't necessary to be so miserable. Reach out for help. You *can* find the peace you crave.

Do you struggle with an addiction such as alcoholism, drug abuse, overeating, gambling, overwork, or overspending? Which one(s)?

_____

_____

Have you ever received treatment or support for this problem?

_____

Are you aware of the shameful and isolated feelings that addictions create?

_____

Would you ever consider asking for help to return to balance?

_____

If not, why not?

_____

If you knew you could receive support and yet remain completely anonymous and safe, would you consider going to a twelve-step recovery group?

PLAY

Our vitality is the domain of the inner child, and one of the most wonderful ways to balance this center is to play. Playing is a lost art in many adults, mostly because we have been indoctrinated to believe it is a waste of time. Nothing could be further from the truth. In fact, genuine play is one of the best possible uses of our time, restoring our physical and sensory being and revitalizing our spirits as well.

We can experience play in many ways. Men often experience it through sports and games, fishing, camping, or watching sports events. For women, play can entail sharing intimacies with friends over lunch, at the makeup counter, or while shopping. Either sex can play while riding a bike, Rollerblading, skiing, or going for a walk. You can take an afternoon off and watch movies or go to a concert, or have dinner with friends. Playing with children is another way to awaken our vitality. One of my favorite ways to boost my vitality is to play charades with my kids, or simply sit around the kitchen telling stories together. Once the kids get going, they are absolutely hilarious, and just goofing around being silly with them is one of the most healing and balancing activities I can think of for my second chakra.

My neighbor Joe insists that, for an evening of fun, nothing is better than a good game of Scrabble with his wife. My friend Jim and his girlfriend love to bowl, and my brother and his wife like to dress up and go dancing. You can also play quietly by working on arts and crafts projects. You can gather a group of friends and play volleyball, have a barbecue, or sit around a piano or a guitar and sing favorite songs. Playing can even be chatting on the phone, sharing laughs with a good friend whom you love dearly.

HOW PLAYFUL ARE YOU?

What is your favorite form of recreation?

_____

When is the last time you played with friends?

_____

What did you do?

_____

_____

How much time do you allow for play or recreation in a week? A month? A year?

_____

Can you remember the last time you had great fun? What were you doing? Who were you with? How did you feel?

_____

_____

Describe the last time you laughed really hard or the last great joke you heard. How did you feel afterward?

_____

_____

 TRY THIS!

Play Games
Invite a few friends over for an evening of games. The more eventful the game, the more fun. Some good choices are Yahtzee, Scrabble, and Twister.

SEXUAL PLAY
One of the most exquisite forms of adult play is found in our sexuality. When we connect with another caring human being and share our most intimate self with them in an atmosphere of safety and appreciation, we balance our second chakra and our hearts as well.

The key to experiencing the healing effects of sexual play is to be in that atmosphere of safety and appreciation. When we open our most vulnerable and sensitive selves to someone who will receive us as a gift, we can heal our very soul. But opening ourselves to someone who doesn't appreciate us can have a devastating effect on our spirit, whether we admit it to ourselves or not. Sexuality is the most powerful expression of our life force, since it gives us the ability to create life itself. My teachers taught me that when we are sexual with someone, our two life forces commingle and remain commingled for weeks. Anyone you have sexual contact with will literally live in your body for that period of time. If that person is someone who cherishes you and holds you as a special and adored person, the commingling of your energies can be empowering and strengthening. If, however, you commingle your life force with someone who is indifferent or uncaring, you may find it painful to live with that energy for any period of time. Like it or not, there really isn't such a thing as casual sex on an energetic level. Sex is a profound and long-lasting interaction that has definite effects on one's spirit.

In our culture, enjoying our sexuality is often a short-lived experience. If we are lucky, some of us do have a lusty period in our lives, usually when we are just discovering our sexuality in our teens and twenties. This is the time when passion abounds and all of life seems erotic. But once we marry and have children, our sexual nature is often traded in for "Mommy and Daddy" energy, which can be all but death to our passionate lives. Our kids seem to psychically sabotage our sexual lives. Can you imagine, for example, telling your kids that tonight you and Daddy want to go to bed early so you two can have fun together?

The thing to remember is that the second chakra is the center of creativity, ingenuity, and desire. You can draw upon all these qualities to create and sustain an exciting sexual life if you decide that you have the right to enjoy that aspect of your nature completely.

Allow yourself to experience your sexuality in every way that is comfortable for you. Explore your sexuality alone and with your beloved, creating the time and space to play in a loving and joyful fashion.

SEXY YOU

Are you comfortable with your sexuality? Do you enjoy feeling and acting sexy?

_____

What is the sexual atmosphere that you set for yourself? Do you create time and privacy for sexual play?

_____

Does your sexual life honor your need for safety and for genuine appreciation?

_____

Most of all, is your sexuality bringing you pleasure?

_____

TRY THIS!

Have a Pillow Fight

The next time you and your partner go to bed, instead of diving into a book or turning on the television, start a pillow fight. Playfully bop your mate on the head with your pillow, and challenge him or her to a battle. A rousing pillow fight is great for just about anyone's inner child and often leads to the most sensual delights.

THE SENSUAL LIFE

Balanced vitality is a way of life. It is a life lived with sensitivity and good taste. It is a life that celebrates beauty, balance, and harmony. It is not about material possessions, although nice things reflect a balanced vitality. It is having an awareness that we are delicate and sensitive creatures who require sweetness, softness, comfort, stimulation, and beauty as much as we require oxygen and food.

Everything in your life—your clothing, your personal grooming, even your home—should reflect this kind of awareness. In fact, feng shui, or the Chinese art of placement, is centered on creating a soothing atmosphere for your second chakra. Environments become charged with energy and take on a personality of their own, much as people do. You can appreciate this when you think of the atmosphere, for example, of a tabernacle or a chapel versus the atmosphere of a hospital or a doctor's office. We experience and absorb the quality of various atmospheres through our feeling center, our sensory center. Whether we realize it or not, these atmospheres have a powerful effect on how we feel, even physically.

You can experiment with this by simply noticing the way your own mood changes as you move from room to room in your own house. Notice how it feels when the atmosphere is beautiful and harmonious, versus when it is disruptive or ugly. Even when we do not consciously register the effect an environment has on us, we still respond to it on an unconscious level. Atmosphere has such a strong impact on me that it actually can affect my health. Whenever I am in an environment that is cozy and warm and sensual, my body responds with gratitude and joy. But when I find myself in an unloved, ugly, dissonant environment, I become irritable and anxious; I can hardly wait to get out of there.

Keep the atmosphere and attitude in your life as beautiful as possible. You have a sensitive energy body that craves and responds to beauty and harmony in every way. Beauty is so important to the human experience that my teacher, Dr. Trenton Tully, once told me that creating beauty is one of the highest and most healing purposes we can pursue.

How conscious are you of the importance of beauty in your life?

_____

What is the most dissonant or ugly facet of your life?

_____

Can you turn this around or restore beauty in any way?

_____

RESTORING VITALITY

When you are *slightly* imbalanced

- See a romantic movie.

- Listen to sensuous music.

- Set the dinner table with your best china and silver, even if you don't have company for dinner.

- Have a glamorous photograph taken of yourself.

- Eat *one* piece of Belgian chocolate.

- Buy yourself a new perfume or aftershave.

- Take a long, sensuous bubble bath by candlelight in your favorite bath oil.

- Buy a comfy bathrobe.

- Wake up at dawn, and watch the sun rise.

- Roast marshmallows in the fireplace with your kids.

- Rock in a rocking chair or swing on a porch swing.

- Visit an amusement park or go to an outdoor concert.

When you are *moderately* imbalanced

- Go to a cabaret, theater, or nightclub and see a play or show. You can also see wonderful theater and dance performances at your local high schools and colleges.

- Send someone (or yourself) a love letter.

- Get both a manicure and a pedicure in one afternoon—this goes for men as well as women.

- If your budget doesn't allow for a professional manicure or pedicure, ask a good friend if he or she would exchange manicures and pedicures with you. (This suggestion counts doubly, because it is also a great way to play with a friend.)

- Wear the best fabrics you can afford.

- Get a weekly massage with aromatherapy.

- Take a walk in the rain, and enjoy getting wet.

- Surround yourself with scented candles and soft classical music.

- Disappear into a good, thick romantic novel.

- Share your favorite bread, cheese, wine, and dessert with a beloved friend.

- Have a potluck dinner with your best friends, and watch a romantic comedy.

- Walk through an arboretum or conservatory while listening to classical music on a Walkman.

- Rent the movie *Bagdad Café* by Percy Adlon.

- Fill your home with flowers, scents, color, and art.

When you have a *major* imbalance

- See a stylist, and get a fabulous new haircut. (Most beauty schools have stylists who will gladly consult with you free of charge because they are always in need of models.)

- Rub a few drops of neroli or patchouli essential oil on the insides of your wrists until they feel warm, and gently inhale the aroma several times a day.

- See a wardrobe consultant, and discover your best personal style. (Most department stores have personal wardrobe consultants on staff who work free of charge.)

- Check into a health spa for a weekend.

- Check into your favorite hotel or a country bed-and-breakfast inn for a weekend. (Watch the travel section in your local newspaper for weekend specials.)

- Go camping for a weekend at the most beautiful site in your area, and bring along delicious food to eat while you are there.

- Beautify your bedroom and bath with a fresh paint job, sensuous art on the walls, and new linens and towels.

- Join a gourmet club, a movie club, or a book club for monthly gatherings.

- Walk, run, bicycle, or Rollerblade along a body of water such as a lake, river, or ocean as often as possible.

- Silently watch the sun set from beginning to end.

- Throw yourself a "Wasn't I great!" party.

- Get the face-lift, tummy tuck, hair transplant, new toupee, laser eye surgery, dental work, etc., you've secretly always wanted. (If you do this, however, go to the best doctor you can find.)

Remember, vitality is

Comfort
Pleasure
Romance
Desire
Beauty
Ingenuity
Passion
Sensuality
Affection
Style
Sexuality
Indulgence
Sweetness

As you regain balance in your vitality chakra, you may be inspired with personal remedies of your own for maintaining balance. Write down all your personal ideas below.

_____

_____

_____

_____

THE THIRD CHAKRA is located in the center of the body, in the solar plexus, halfway between the navel and the rib cage. This chakra governs the sphere of self-direction, personal will and intention, physical energy, and self-control. This energy station affects our self-esteem and how we feel about ourselves. It reflects our ability to accept responsibility for ourselves and assume personal authority over our lives. It is the center for our personal expression of power. In the color spectrum, it vibrates energetically to the color yellow, like a noonday sun.

Third Chakra

Balanced Sovereignty

If the second chakra is the domain of our inner child, the third chakra is the domain of our intellect and our inner adult. Once our vitality is awakened and our balance is solidly established in the second chakra, we are then able to travel energetically upward into this third center of energy, where we begin to decide which direction we want to move toward in life. Being the domain of personal sovereignty, the third chakra, when functioning properly, endows us with the intention and strength to stay true to our course, giving us the ability to become "captain of our own ship" and ruler of our own experience. We can identify what is necessary and important to us in life and choose to support it without compromise.

On a physiological level, this chakra governs the stomach, pancreas, adrenals, upper intestines, gallbladder, and liver as well as the lower back, located behind the solar plexus. When your third chakra is imbalanced, you may experience problems with these areas of your body. Intellectually, this energy station determines our level of decision, direction, and personal leadership; emotionally, it infuses our willingness and ability to trust our intuition and take the risks that go along with leading a personally satisfying life.

Our personal sovereignty also governs our self-image and how we imagine ourselves to be perceived by the world. Through this center, we develop our personalities and decide who we want to be. This is where we choose our masks in life, assume our characters, and meet the world. Its mission statement is "I choose. I intend. I rule. I will." Our personal sovereignty awakens us to the realization that we ultimately direct the course of our lives. It shifts us out of dependency on others for our happiness and places it squarely on our own shoulders.

YOUR INNER BELIEFS

Your third chakra determines the beliefs you hold about yourself. Those are the statements you tell yourself, such as "I'm successful," "I'm a victim," "I'm a helper," "I'm a worker bee," "I'm an artist." It's where your personality takes on its character. If your power is balanced, you will feel confident and worthy, and you will be able to make decisions that support your path in the best possible way. You will be able to focus on your true heart's desires and choose behaviors and actions that fully align with your intentions. Balanced sovereignty will keep you faithful to what is important to your emotional, physical, and spiritual well-being. It will give you the stamina and motivation to stay your course no matter what is going on around you.

Strong personal sovereignty establishes a healthy self-esteem, derived from your determination to fully trust your own instincts and act on them without compromise. It invokes a high degree of self-awareness and self-examination, which lays the groundwork for solid integrity and the capacity to trust. This center is the point of origin of your most fundamental intuitions, inviting you to take charge of your life and follow your hunches and guiding impulses completely. It is the source of determination and conviction. Without such power, we would never be able to lead the kind of life we really want.

Personal sovereignty is also the impetus of personal motivation. Related to the life force of the sun itself, this center invigorates your physical body with life force and stimulates your ability to willfully take action when necessary and follow through. This center dictates choice, decision, commitment, ethics, integrity, responsibility, and action.

COURAGE

When you establish personal sovereignty, you have the ability to stand up against adversaries and oppressors and fight for your rights. This center is sometimes known as the warrior's chakra because it encompasses the ability to say no at times, to fight back, to set limits, to become angry, to confront invasions, and to face down and stop whatever and whoever dishonors you, no matter how fearful you may be.

One example of the power of personal sovereignty is Steven's experience. Steven had just had back surgery and was slowly on the mend. Restless from sitting, he decided one evening to walk to a friend's house, a little over a block away. Minutes after leaving his friend's house to return home, he felt as though he were being watched. Sure enough, his suspicions were confirmed as a man walking on the other side of the street switched over to his side and followed at an ominous pace behind him. His first thought was "Uh-oh. I can't run. I'm going to get robbed. I'm going to get ambushed." But then he remembered what I taught him about the power of personal sovereignty and put it to the test. He placed his hand over his third chakra and started to envision it getting bigger and bigger and stronger and stronger, creating a protective shield around him. Seconds later, he heard footsteps running behind him, but before the man caught up to him, Steven, feeling completely empowered, spun around and confronted his assailant first, not even noticing that he had a gun pointing at him. With the adrenaline flowing and feeling totally in charge in his third chakra, Steven shouted without thinking, "You stop that! You're gonna get in trouble! Now get out of here!" The assailant was so shocked and overwhelmed by Steven's sudden and unexpected show of force that he lowered the gun and ran off.

POWER CREATES PEACE

Sovereignty is the center of power and strength—yet paradoxically, when it is balanced, it endows one with serenity, gentleness, and patience. This is because it frees us of the fear of others, which causes us to be aggressive, defensive, and harsh. A person who is truly sovereign is a peacemaker because he or she does not feel threatened by others. When we remain faithful to our priorities, we naturally become more appreciative and respectful of the needs and desires of others because we understand their importance to personal well-being. If we are accountable to ourselves, we will become accountable to others.

Balanced sovereignty matures us in our awareness that we are not the only one on the planet; we must cooperate and live in harmony with others. True power arises from an ability to accept our interdependence upon one another and to realize that we are all in this life together. It takes us further than our selfish whims, especially those founded on our childish notions that others are responsible for our happiness, and it shows us the need for compromise, collaboration, and generosity. It helps us recognize that everyone has the same right to personal fulfillment that we do and that no one has the time or ability to do our work for us. This level of accountability takes us out of the "victim" mode and provides us the tools to fulfill our own requirements. Such self-reliance is at the core of any real and lasting power and personal peace of mind.

How peaceful are you?

Do you ever feel as though others "owe you one"?

_____

Are you willing and able to be accountable for your own personal peace?

_____

_____

Are you presently engaged in any spoken or unspoken battles or power struggles? With whom?

_____

_____

Are you a troublemaker? Do you stir up battles to get others to do things for you?

_____

THE RELATIONSHIP CENTER

With personal sovereignty, we awaken and strengthen our ability to take a stand and live according to our ethics and values. Balanced power endows us with self-reliance, good concentration, focused intention, confidence, and a well-directed sense of being in control of our own destiny, all of which are essential for success. This chakra assists us in finding the courage to listen to, trust, and act on our hunches. A person with such a genuine sense of power is usually charismatic and has a compelling and attractive quality about them. Such people often assume leadership roles early in life.

Because our personal sovereignty plays such a major role in how we relate to the world, it is the energy center that most influences our relationships with others, both on a personal and on a professional level. Genuine relationships depend first on a healthy relationship with our selves. If we do not have a strong and appreciative sense of our worth and value in the world, neither will others. True power lies in our ability to accept ourselves—the good, the bad, and the "ugly"—and to not project our shadow side onto those around us. It allows us to embrace and accept the private "I," which includes at times the fearful, weak, lazy, manipulative, childish "I" behind our public personas. This is not to indulge or make excuses for these sabotaging aspects of ourselves, but rather to acknowledge that they exist and need to be overcome. My teachers have always said that denying our weaknesses is neither power nor protection. We cannot overcome those disabling parts of our own nature, which in fact steal our power away, if we do not acknowledge that they exist. Until we do so, we are not fully in charge of our destiny. Just as an army is only as strong as its weakest link, so too are we only as strong as our own personal weaknesses. Until we recognize them, we cannot endeavor to strengthen them. At this level of consciousness, we step into our spiritual maturity and own that this is our life and no one else's to live. When we embrace our weaknesses and begin to work on our personal development, we feel our power and its full potential to express and manifest in this lifetime. Life becomes exciting and takes on a real sense of adventure and wonder.

What parts of your own personality are you unhappy with?

_____

_____

Are you a victim? Do you feel the world is out to get you?

_____

_____

Are you a perfectionist? Do you feel you must hide your weaknesses or keep people from getting too close?

_____

_____

Are you taking any steps to confront those parts of your nature or personality that need improvement?

_____

_____

Have you ever thought about or received mentoring or counseling to help you grow and overcome your weaknesses?

_____

_____

POWER AND CONTROL

Whenever you enter into a psychic agreement with someone that suggests that they are more powerful than you are, sovereignty shuts down. You surrender your personal power and actually turn it over to the bullies, allowing them to use it against you. At times you may be aware of this agreement, such as when you continue to work in a hostile environment, even though you know it isn't healthy for you to stay. Most of the time, however, people are unconscious of these disabling agreements. These types of oppressed third chakra experiences are the foundation of most codependencies and addiction-based relationships.

When you shut down your third chakra out of fear of something or someone, your body literally loses power as well. Your adrenals begin to pump, your heart races, your stomach balls up in knots, and you hold your breath, all of which physically weaken you. We've all faced these kinds of situations, such as when the intimidating boss calls you in, or the abusive neighbor starts complaining, or the doctor only grunts at you instead of giving you his full and respectful attention. At these times, when we feel threatened and overwhelmed, the third chakra, which governs the fight-or-flight syndrome, prepares us for the worst.

This is the case, for example, in battered housewife syndrome or, even more distressing, in child abuse—a violation especially common in homes where drugs and alcohol prevail. I had a client, Mim, who was a very hardworking and talented real estate developer. She had a real knack for buying run-down properties, renovating them, and then reselling them. She made a fortune over time and was well respected in the real estate community. And yet despite her success in business, Mim was a battered, abused, and terrified wife in her marriage to an alcoholic attorney. Even though she had vision and brains, he constantly harassed her about her business deals, accusing her of being incompetent, insisting that she turn over every dime she made, flying into rages on a whim, calling her names, and on occasion even striking her. Even though she had proven herself capable of financial self-reliance, she was paralyzed and unable to break away. She had been raised to believe that a good wife is compliant and submits to her husband.

Unfortunately, Mim's husband was neither balanced nor fair; he was a greedy, addicted, and ambitious man who was dangerous to be around. As undeniably clear as it was to her that she should divorce him, her personal sovereignty was so diminished that she couldn't take a single step out the door. Not until he broke her nose did her rebellion finally kick in. She went to a battered women's support group, got a personal therapist, and hired the best attorney she could find. And still it was a tremendous struggle for her to stay in her power. Finally she took a self-defense course. Getting physically stronger allowed her psychic defenses to kick in. Two years later, after the divorce was finalized, her ex-husband developed terminal liver disease. In retrospect she can't understand why she was so afraid of him and withstood so much abuse. It wasn't because he was himself that powerful. Seeing him in his disabled state, she realized that he was even weaker and more afraid of life than she. "Now that I've learned to own my power, I'm not afraid of much of anything," she said. "He provoked me into getting stronger, and I'm grateful to him for the provocation, because now I'm genuinely peaceful and no longer afraid."

Are you living in fear of anyone or anything? Who? What?

_____

_____

Do you feel as though you must submit to the demands or behavior of anyone you live with?

_____

Have you ever taken any steps to empower yourself in the face of those who intimidate you?

_____

Have you ever taken a self-defense course? How would you defend yourself if you were to find yourself in danger?

_____

Are you a bully? Do you demand that others submit to you? Are you intruding on another's sovereign rights?

_____

_____

HOW DID I LOSE MY POWER?

Often people ask, "How did I lose my power?" Some of us, like Mim, were taught to surrender to outside authorities when we were very young. Of course, this is both wise and necessary when we are infants and toddlers, innocent about the dangers of the world, but as we age, we should gradually be given more opportunity to exercise our power and direct our own course. When we are made to submit to power for its own sake, and not for any sensible reason, our sovereignty becomes stunted.

When that occurs, we live in fear, ignore our instincts, and fail to respond to our true callings in life for fear of rejection, disapproval, or abandonment. These, after all, were the consequences we suffered as children.

The emotional consequences of a weak sovereignty are codependency (the condition in which pleasing others is more important than pleasing ourselves), depression, addiction, and suppressed anger. These can result in digestive problems, ulcers, irritable colon, gallbladder problems, excessive weight around the middle, and loss of appetite. Our spiritual loss is the inability to live in our truth and be who we really are.

CHECKING YOUR PERSONAL POWER

	Yes	No	Sometimes
Can you say no easily?	——	——	——
Are you able to make commitments and stick with them?	——	——	——
Do you speak your mind openly and without fear?	——	——	——
Do you honor your body's needs (i.e., sleep when tired, eat when hungry, rest when fatigued)?	——	——	——
Are you mutually respectful in your personal relationships?	——	——	——

	Yes	No	Sometimes
Are you able to communicate your needs clearly and honestly?	___	___	___
Can you allow others to be unhappy or uncomfortable without trying to rescue them?	___	___	___
Do you do as much for yourself as you do for others?	___	___	___
Are you able to stop intrusions before "blowing up" or getting excessively angry?	___	___	___
Can you address authority figures without being afraid?	___	___	___
Are you honestly doing what you want to do in life?	___	___	___
Do you feel satisfied with the choices you are making in your life?	___	___	___
Do you involve yourself with things that are important to you?	___	___	___
Do you have supportive friends?	___	___	___
Do you feel in charge of your life?	___	___	___
Do you feel able to take care of yourself?	___	___	___
Do you feel that you are safe in your relationships?	___	___	___

If you answered no to any one of these questions, your sovereignty is somewhat imbalanced. If you answered no to two or three questions, you are slightly imbalanced and should follow the suggestions for slight imbalances at the end of the chapter. If you answered no to four to seven questions, then you are moderately imbalanced and should follow the suggestions for adjusting moderate imbalances. If you answered no to eight or more questions, then your sovereignty is seriously shut down. You should follow the suggestions for serious imbalances in order to heal and enjoy life more.

TAKING YOUR POWER BACK

If our personal sovereignty is out of balance, it is difficult to heal this energy center entirely on our own. We need the support and help of others to end the isolation that feeds our weakness. Some people, however, are so sensitive to others that even when they want to strengthen their personal boundaries, they find it hard to separate what is theirs from what is not. If this is the case for you, you may need to engage support while you work on becoming stronger and less available.

I had a client, Jennie, who was a massage therapist. She scheduled a reading with me because she was having a financial crisis. She could not manage to pay her bills or support herself, in spite of the fact that she worked very hard. Instead she was exhausted, in debt, and angry. My reading showed that Jennie's sovereignty was nonexistent, resulting in others constantly trampling on her. Friends would often ask her for free massages, which she would agree to, even though she didn't want to. When clients complained about the price of her sessions—she was a tremendous healer and charged a very reasonable price for her work— she would immediately respond by allowing them to pay what they wanted, which was frequently nothing. Others showed up late for appointments without canceling or, worse, didn't show up at all. When she would contact them wondering where they were, they offered only lame excuses.

In addition to her poor business practices, Jennie was surrounded by a sea of complainers who often telephoned asking her for last-minute favors, or money, or simply to listen to their problems, which, of course, she did. No wonder she was broke, overwhelmed, and exhausted. She was running a cut-rate massage therapy practice with a "Dial-a-Crisis" service on the side. She justified her inability to say no by telling herself what a "good, giving person" she was. But the truth was that, underneath it all, she was depressed, angry, and resentful of every person who intruded upon her. Mostly, however, she was angry with herself for being such a pushover.

A pacifist by nature, she lacked the ability to draw her boundaries. She found confronting people so upsetting, their energy so overwhelming, that in the turbulent energy of the moment, she would forget her focus and strive only to make peace. That is, at least, until later, when she would have a delayed reaction and become furious.

Given Jennie's nature, I advised that she become realistic and try another course of action. Because she was so dreadfully ineffective in maintaining her own boundaries and would probably remain so, I suggested that she hire a secretary to do it for her. That way someone else could be the "heavy," while she maintained her sweet demeanor and energetic requirements for calm. As radical as it felt, and as nervous as Jennie was about being able to afford it, she did take my advice and hired someone that week. The entire drama soon turned around. The secretary had no trouble establishing limits, and Jennie's business shaped up in a hurry. People realized that unless they were respectful of both her time and her talent, they couldn't get to see her at all. With the help of her secretary, Jennie and her clients learned together to respect her. With her new boundaries established and her sovereignty moving into place, Jennie realized that she was just a student when it came to learning about power, but at least she was now moving in the right direction.

List three ways in which you allow yourself to be intruded upon.

1. _____

2. _____

3. _____

List three ways in which you can choose to establish your boundaries and respect yourself.

1. _____

2. _____

3. _____

You can tell if your third chakra is weak by how smoothly life runs and how respected and confident you feel. You can also evaluate your third chakra by determining how much anger or frustration you need to manage and how peaceful you feel with your own choices. Most of all, you can evaluate your balance of power by how well your personal boundaries are established.

How respected do you feel?

_____

Are you angry or insecure?

_____

Are your boundaries clear and maintained?

_____

BREATH IS POWER

Sara, another client, also struggled with weak sovereignty and had what she called the "I'm in trouble" syndrome. Married over twenty-five years to a wealthy but mean-spirited bully who was much like her father, she found secret support on the Internet by joining a chat group of other oppressed housewives. One day her husband came home early from work and found her on the Net; he saw what her group was about and threw a fit. He forbade her to use the computer ever again. Of course, the minute he left for work the next day, she was right back at it, taking even more delight in her secret rebellion.

All went undiscovered until one day, minutes before her husband was due to arrive home, the computer crashed. Panicking, she started to have an anxiety attack. Then she remembered a woman from the chat group, and the information she had shared with everyone from a class she took in regaining personal power. According to this woman, whenever you feel threatened or afraid, you should place your hands over your third chakra, right in the middle of your stomach, and breathe very deliberately and slowly until you feel calm. In doing so, you will actually begin to feel stronger and more protected. Breath gives us life, and it is the source of our power. When we become afraid, we often hold our breath, even without realizing it, which diminishes our life force and power. The way to counteract this is to remain very conscious of our breath and to steadily breathe through any anxiety-provoking experience, real or imagined, until our balance and power return. Sara had thought this technique seemed far-fetched and silly, but now desperate, she tried it. She covered her midriff with her right hand and focused on calming down, breathing deeply and regularly, without interruption. In a few short moments, she actually began to feel better. Thrilled, she continued to breathe through her urgency and tried pressing a few keys on the computer. After a try or two, the computer came to life again. Breathing a sigh of relief, she signed off seconds before her husband pulled into the driveway.

Exhilarated by that experience and her newfound tool for staying in her power, she repeated the exercise at other moments when she felt scared or intimidated by him. More and more, her fear began to fade in the face of his outbursts, and he began to seem less threatening. Soon she began to ignore rather than react to his berating comments. At times she actually found him amusing. It took only two weeks of practicing this simple technique before she broke through the hurtful pattern of interaction that had gone on for over twenty-five years. Her determined breathing kept her free of the fear and stress that she used to feel every time he got angry, and gave her a new life.

TRY THIS!

A Forceful Expulsion

When someone disrespects you and you feel threatened, take charge of the situation by placing your hands over your solar plexus and envisioning your third chakra becoming stronger and warmer, until it completely fills your aura. Next, fill your lungs to capacity and, with your hands still on your third chakra, envision the offensive person in your mind's eye. Then breathe out as hard and as forcefully as you can, almost as if you are snorting, while imagining you are actually exhaling the offender and pushing him or her out of your personal space. Though this exercise may leave you feeling uncomfortable, it is just this kind of forcefulness that expands the third chakra and establishes your limits. When you do this exercise, you empower your third chakra and you expel the unwanted or invading energy.

TRY THIS!

The Golden Disk

This remedy is a martial arts technique for balancing and awakening the third chakra. Whenever you are afraid or need to enhance your willpower, stand up, take in a deep breath, and put your hand just under the ribs on your solar plexus. Slowly envision a golden disk covering this area of your body. Imagine that this disk can deflect any harmful energy that is intentionally or unintentionally directed at you and protect you completely from any upset. Breathe in slowly as you do this.

Continue this exercise for at least two minutes, longer if possible, until you feel calm and totally relaxed and begin to feel your power once again.

 TRY THIS!

Protect Your Solar Plexus

A variation of the Golden Disk is to subtly fold your hands over your solar plexus, the area of your third chakra, whenever you are speaking with someone you fear or who has a negative or upsetting effect on you, in order to protect yourself. Better yet, position your body so that you do not face them directly; this will prevent their energy from invading your energy field through the solar plexus. This remedy works wonders for me when I am working with an excessively emotional client. It allows me to observe without absorbing their energy, so I can work with them and guide them without falling into their negativity. It can also work for you, especially if you are dealing with a difficult person or find yourself feeling intimidated in any way. As an added measure of protection, as you interact, send kind and loving thoughts their way, just to let him or her know that you are no threat.

LAUGHTER IS THE BEST MEDICINE

Another incredible tonic for a weak third chakra is to laugh at life, especially at those things that you feel are oppressing you, intimidating you, and keeping you from being your true self.

My speech teacher in high school used to suggest that if we were ever scared or intimidated by an audience, to just imagine everybody sitting in their seats in their underwear. The image made us all laugh and put the world back into perspective. We lost our fear and usually did a fine job of public speaking.

Once you laugh at something, it ceases to have power over you. I discovered this in first grade, when I was dreadfully afraid of our school principal, Sister Mary Norbert. She was an enormous somber German nun who never smiled, and she scared every child in the school. In the spring of my first grade year, during our school carnival, my girlfriend Susie tripped with her taffy apple in her hand and fell against Sister Norbert's back. Her apple stuck to Sister's veil. As she attempted to pull it off, the entire veil came along with it, exposing Sister's nearly bald head. The situation was so hilarious to me that I fell on the floor laughing. Flustered, Sister turned and ran into the office to regroup—she never even noticed me laughing so hard. From that moment on, I could never look at Sister Norbert again and be afraid.

If you find yourself feeling weak, intimidated, or even too invested in a situation, consciously seek out ways to make yourself laugh. You can achieve this by going to the movies or renting a funny movie. You can achieve it by going to a comedy club with a friend, or picking up a hilarious book, or seeing a theatrical farce or comedy. One of my mother's favorite sayings is "The situation is critical, but not serious." In other words, any intimidating situation becomes more manageable with a dose of humor.

TRY THIS!

Check Out Humor
The next time you find yourself feeling totally overwhelmed and humorless, go to your local library and check out the humor and comedy sections in the movie department. There you will find classic comedies such as *It's a Mad Mad Mad Mad World*, with Ethel Merman and Phil Silvers, and *Waiting for Guffman*, with Christopher Guest. You will also find old Jackie Gleason *Honeymooners* episodes, *I Love Lucy* reruns with Lucille Ball, and all the Marx Brothers movies. Usually librarians have insider tips on more obscure comedies as well, so don't hesitate to ask for recommendations while you are there.

TOO MUCH OF A GOOD THING
Just as a lack of sovereignty presents problems, so too does overcompensating in an attempt to balance this energy. Our power center can get overinflated when we try to gain some control in our lives. Overcompensating can leave a person narrow-minded, too linear in his or her thinking, relentless, unyielding, and fixed. In extreme cases, one can become

intimidating, overbearing, aggressive, and insensitive. Our competitive society actually values these qualities and considers them desirable. People who have an overinflated third chakra often end up in positions of great leadership, with power and influence over others.

From the perspective of worldly accomplishments and acquisition, having a hyperactive third chakra is advantageous. From a broader perspective, however, an overinflated power center causes problems, in that people become workaholic or too dogmatic and oppressive. Those whose power center is stuck on "high" also tend to suffer from strained relationships due to having linear and exclusive points of view; they often lack awareness of other people and situations. Though they are unquestionably "doers" in life, they often feel that their concerns are the only ones that are important. People with overinflated power centers are often as driven by fear as people with weak centers, but rather than allowing life to oppress them, they choose to grab life by the horns. This is generally a more desirable way to live, except when your grip on the horns becomes so tight that you do not dare to let go. When that happens, you begin to narrow your range of experiences considerably.

Another indication of an overinflated power center is an overbearing personality. An expanded energy field does have a strong influence on others, but often in undesirable ways. Sometimes this imbalance reveals itself in subtle and manipulative behaviors, such as using flattery and gift giving and always being the nice guy (unless crossed), in order to gain quiet control over others and consequently feel safe.

Expanded sovereignty compels one to be extremely hardworking, and the accomplishments of people with this type of energy can be impressive. They also find at least a semblance of control in being the "doer" rather than the "follower." Not surprisingly, many are workaholics, who use their work as a way to avoid uncomfortable feelings or to prove their worthiness to themselves and others. The truth is these people do not run their lives—they are run by life. They must struggle to slow down or relax. While this may sound terrible and you would wonder who would want to live like this, someone you like or admire very much does so. It may be the principal who runs the high school, the coach who manages the baseball team, or the secretary who never misses a day of work, rain or shine. They are really their own worst enemies. I know because I am one of these people.

I find that my own power center has a very strong tendency to become overinflated because as a child I was always rewarded for being the "good girl who worked so hard." Like many kids, I was afraid of being found unworthy of love and respect. Probably because I was one of seven siblings, I discovered early in life that a good way to get attention was to become the "worker bee." I became quite accomplished and enjoyed getting good grades, being the best student, best cheerleader, best raffle-ticket salesman, best baby-sitter, or the best at whatever assignment came my way. I liked the sense of power, control, and attention it gave me to "do, do, do" and do it well. Unfortunately that "doer" thermostat can get stuck, and now I find I must temper my own work ethic and learn to relax, especially since I absolutely love my work. But I also love my family, and they get tired of my work; they want me to be just as interested in their lives and priorities as I am in mine, and rightfully so. When it comes to balancing my third chakra, my children are my teachers. They demand my interest in their lives; they want me to play with them and let loose the reins of life once in a while. They are right. Real power and confidence lie in realizing the limits of what we can do as much as it lies in doing what we can. My teacher once said to me, "Sometimes the most powerful thing you can do in life is nothing."

Are you a workaholic or an overachiever?

_____

Are you able to relax and enjoy life from time to time? How?

_____

_____

What do you like to do when you are not working? How often do you do this?

_____

_____

POWER OF CHOICE

Because the third chakra has to do with willpower and our ability to direct our own lives, one of the most powerful ways to strengthen our sovereignty is to realize that no matter what we face in life, our greatest power is the power of choice. No matter who appears to exert control over us, at some point our own agreement to go along with this oppression causes us to become oppressed. Life can dictate that we suffer physical restrictions and limitations, but no one has the ability to restrict or in any way demean our spirit unless we agree to it.

One of the most poignant illustrations of the power of the third chakra is the now-famous haunting image of a single unarmed student standing up to an entire battalion of Chinese tanks in Tiananmen Square during the 1989 student uprising. Using just the power of his convictions, he was not only not crushed, but in fact was able to stop the tanks dead in their tracks. Students like him were able to turn the army on its heels. The soldiers retreated from the square and did not return for two more weeks.

What three choices can you make today to feel more sovereignty in your life?

_____

At work?

_____

At home?

_____

With friends?

_____

 TRY THIS!

Try On Another Role

The next time you are alone with someone you don't know, try acting like someone you've always wanted to be. For example, if your personality is low key and shy, just for the duration of your time with the stranger, be gregarious and outgoing. Or if you are loud and aggressive, pretend you are calm and serene. If you are really adventurous, you can even pretend that you are in a profession other than your own. I've been criticized for advocating this technique for balancing the third chakra: it looks as if I'm encouraging people to lie. But my argument is that whatever comes out of us is a real and true part of us. The point is not to deceive but to be playful. Every child under the age of ten will tell you how much fun it is to pretend to be someone other than yourself. Lighten up, and remember how enjoyable this can be. It's also very liberating for those who are crusted over in their old, uninteresting personalities and don't know how to get out of them.

INTEGRITY

Another factor in balancing your third chakra is being honest about your intentions and motives. So many times we find ourselves in compromising situations because we initiate something without much commitment and then expect others to bail us out. For example, I met a young chiropractor who had started a healing center in Minneapolis and surrounded himself with a very fine group of alternative practitioners. Yet in spite of his terrific initial burst of enthusiasm, Dr. Morris constantly complained that he didn't make enough money. He wanted the practitioners to take pay cuts, work overtime, and bring in more business. All the while, he himself showed up less and less, expecting them to carry the ball. Not surprisingly, the workers caught on to his mixed commitment, and one by one, they quit. The center went bankrupt in less than two years. Dr. Morris just couldn't understand how things had gone so wrong. He was resentful of his colleagues and very outspoken about it. Unfortunately, this only made him look worse in the eyes of his peers and patients. One night, in a moment of truth, he admitted to another client of mine that he secretly hated chiropractic and had entered into the profession to please his father. "I guess it served me right that I went bankrupt," he said. "Maybe it's a blessing. I've been thinking about studying to be a landscape architect, something I've always wanted to do. Now I can get on with it."

What are you really committed to at this time?

_____

_____

What are your obstacles?

_____

_____

What are you willing to do to support your goals?

_____

_____

How serious are you in being responsible to your dreams?

_____

Are you remaining faithful to your choices and commitments?

_____

THE BALANCING BAR OF THE SPIRIT

Our sovereignty is the balancing bar of our life. It draws our foundation and creativity into the world; it announces who we are and what we intend to do in life. This center energizes us to take action toward those ideals and beliefs that most inspire us. It is the engine that drives our personal power. If the engine breaks down, our lives go nowhere. If your sovereignty is weak and you are passive, lethargic, fatigued, uninterested, and disengaged with your own life, wake yourself up. No one else will live your life for you. Living according to someone else's ideals is a colossal waste of time because they won't appreciate it, nor will this choice reward you in any way, now or in some imagined future. The price you pay for surrendering sovereignty is nothing short of psychic death. Pay attention. Look outward. Be in the moment. Stop. Look. Listen to the world around you. Wherever you are hiding in your thoughts, snap out of it. Do not let the ghosts of your past, or the frightful imaginings of a phantom future, steal away your today and the power it holds for you to be all that you are destined to be. Take your power back. After all, only you can do this.

SURRENDER TO A HIGHER POWER

As you move closer to a balanced personal sovereignty, you will discover that the highest form of personal power is found in surrendering your own limited power to a Higher Power and asking the Universe to direct your course. It is important to take responsibility for doing your part in achieving happiness. Sometimes, however, we severely limit ourselves by clinging to the belief that success is having things the way we want to have them and that anything less is a failure. This perspective restricts our power because it does not allow the Universe to assist us. My teachers taught me that in using willpower, we might ask the Universe for what we want, but we should never presume to tell the Universe how to deliver it. Our limited view simply cannot see our highest good. I cringe at the times I wanted certain love affairs or jobs to work out in my favor, only to realize later that there could have been nothing worse for me than to have gotten my wish. Thank God my mother always taught me to pray for the fulfillment of my request or "better." Gratefully, I can report that I always received the "better."

If you want to experience the greatest power there is, consciously practice surrendering your own personal efforts, and ask the Universe to work on your behalf. Remember your true nature is Divine, a child of God. All of the Universe loves you and wants to help you experience the most beautiful life possible. Cease to question your worthiness once and for all, and open yourself to receiving Divine intervention. Focus your will on your Creator, and surrender your dreams into God's hands. Trust that the Universe has a better, brighter, more wonderful plan for you than any you could ever have conceived of yourself. As the saying goes, "If God is with you, who is against you? For there is no greater power than God."

Living under the direction of Divine Power requires that we surrender all personal control and take a deliberate leap of faith, suspending our need for guarantees of any kind. This will be far easier if we are committed, honest, and faithful to what is important to our hearts and do not expect anyone else to take care of us. When we show up fully to our heart's desire and do everything possible to bring our heads and feet into alignment with our heart, then the Universe also commits. But until we do our part, the Universe can't help. When we direct our will fully toward what lies in our heart, the Universe will meet us halfway, leading us to victory.

RESTORING POWER

 When you are *slightly* imbalanced

- Write a mission statement.

- Reaffirm who you are by practicing writing your name in your most beautiful penmanship.

- Put a lock on your bedroom door.

- Sleep on things before you commit to them.

- Practice saying no.

- Rent the movie *Seven Samurai* by Akira Kurosawa or *The Man Who Would Be King* by John Huston.

- Get a daily planner, and use it.

- Write down your daily goals every morning.

- Write down your accomplishments every night.

- Place affirmations and motivational statements on the bathroom mirror and the dashboard of your car, and read them out loud.

- Get your own personalized coffee or tea cup.

- Give yourself and others compliments freely, and admire rather than hold jealousy.

- Take yourself out on a special date at least once a month.

- Attend an exciting sporting event or competition.

- Read books on time management and leadership.

When you are *moderately* imbalanced

- Take a guilt-free, well-deserved, and long-desired vacation.

- Enroll in a class, and go for an A.

- Start a project, and finish it.

- Hire a personal trainer.

- Read biographies of powerful people whom you admire.

- Respect your competition, and seek models of excellence in people who are stronger or more accomplished than you are.

- Create contracts with yourself, and follow through step by step.

- Paint your office or work space yellow (the color of power and motivation), and put sunflowers on your desk.

- Become the block representative in your neighborhood, or join the condo board of directors.

- Play tennis or racquetball.

- Take an assertiveness training course.

- Learn to belly dance.

- Burn incense to intentionally create a sacred atmosphere.

- Get Caller ID, and screen your phone calls.

- Say your name, out loud, over and over, until you feel you own it.

When you are *seriously* imbalanced

- Go on a vision quest.

- Take up boxing, karate, or tai chi at the local YMCA.

- When speaking about difficult or challenging matters, speak clearly and breathe deeply, taking your time if necessary.

- Eat foods high in carbohydrates that can provide instant energy.

- Find a role model or a "can-do" mentor, and ask them to guide you.

- Hire a personal motivational coach, or get a sponsor through a twelve-step program.

- Share your plans only with those who will support you.

- Take an "improv" or acting class.

- Read and do the exercises in my book *Your Heart's Desire*.

- Train for a marathon or a walk for cancer, and then do it.

- Listen to motivational audiotapes.

- See a career or relationship counselor.

- Start and follow a twenty-minute daily exercise regimen.

- Volunteer for community service, such as teaching adults to read, and continue for at least three months.

- Do all you can, and then surrender to Higher Power.

Personal sovereignty is

Focus
Commitment
Boundaries
Authority
Cooperation
Integrity
Choice
Decision
Discipline
Courage
Faith
Intention
Willingness
Peace
Autonomy

As you regain balance in your third chakra, you will become inspired in ways of your own to maintain this balance. As these ideas present themselves to you, write them down in the space below.

_____

_____

_____

_____

_____

_____

_____

_____

_____

_____

_____

_____

Fourth Chakra

Balanced Heart

THE FOURTH CHAKRA is located near the heart, in the center of the chest. This center, when awakened and balanced, governs our feelings of compassion, forgiveness, understanding, generosity, empathy, caring, and love. The heart is the domain of human intimacy; it activates affection, warmth, nurturing, friendship, and familiarity. On an energy level, it connects the lower ego or physical self to the higher soul or spiritual self. Just as the heart is the most important organ in the body, so too is the fourth chakra, our spiritual heart center, the most important energy center in our psychic makeup. This is because love is the greatest power in our lives and the highest channel of life force available to us. On the color spectrum, this center vibrates energetically to the color green. Its mission statement is "I give. I care. I receive. I love."

The heart is the seat of the soul, our spiritual and Divine Essence. Once we establish and balance our personal sovereignty, we are then able to travel energetically upward into this fourth center of energy, where we begin to open our heart and connect with our fellow man. It is here in the fourth chakra that we are endowed with the capacity to feel joy, unity, laughter, and love, and can share these blessings with those around us. It stimulates our highest ideals and desires, not only for our own good, but for the good of others and the world. When our heart is balanced and open, we feel a genuine sense of flow through our lives, affirming our well-being and spiritual purpose on Earth. We realize our connection to all that is, and we begin in the deepest sense to trust others and ourselves. When our heart center is balanced, we are able to partake of and share in all that the Universe has provided.

On the emotional plane, the heart is the domain of understanding, empathy, and concern for our fellow man. Being the center of love, the heart chakra is naturally associated with family, lovers, friends, spiritual family, and even animals. When it is open and balanced, we care how we affect others and want to touch them in a positive and nurturing way. This energy center encourages us to shift away from the frame of mind "me against the world" toward a more generous and friendly "me as part of the world" outlook. We establish rapport with those around us, value their point of view, and feel compassion and empathy for them, wanting as much for others as we do for ourselves. The fourth chakra is the center of touch and nurturing, and it awakens our desire to be held and cared for. It expresses itself in affection and kindness.

On a physiological level, this center governs the heart, circulation, breasts, arteries, and blood flow. When our heart chakra is balanced, our blood circulation flows smoothly, our heart rhythm is regular, and our arteries are open. The health of our physical heart and breasts is greatly influenced by our spiritual heart center. Many people who have difficulty giving and receiving love freely, or who feel unloved, also suffer from breast and heart diseases or disabilities. When your spiritual heart is closed, you feel heavy in the chest; your breathing is labored, or you take in too much oxygen.

The heart center expands our capacity to be generous, sensitive, kind, merciful, forgiving, tolerant, and emotionally tender. It opens our ability to see into the hearts of those around us and recognize the goodness in all people, even when their behavior isn't considerate. Such love is evident in the parent who loves her child even when he is throwing terrible tantrums or the spouse who loves his alcoholic partner. When we have an open heart, we overlook others' faults and celebrate their strengths.

RESONANCE

When our heart center is balanced, we actually establish energetic resonance with others, entering into a common vibration. When we are on the same energetic wavelength with others, we communicate on a higher level than words allow. We enter into an energetic rapport that is based on complete understanding and acceptance of one another. We've all had these spontaneous heart-based connections, such as when we encounter someone we instantly like or feel as though we've known in the past. In fact, such rapport is often the gateway to love relationships. Do you remember the excitement you felt when you first met your beloved? How you actually thought of the same things at the same time and didn't even need to speak? When this occurs, you are definitely connecting on a heart level.

Because of its attractive and magnetic qualitites, an open and balanced heart center creates synchronicities that seem to fill your every need. The Universe is a hologram aware of all of its parts at all times, and when we move into our heart chakra, we shift into this holographic vibration. This allows the Universe to fill any void that we may be experiencing in our life, giving us exactly what we need, bringing us our heart's desire.

The heart chakra awakens a profound realization of our place in the larger scheme of things; it also governs harmony, balance, and global perspective. As the heart opens, we begin to comprehend that even though we have physical bodies, we are in fact spiritual beings, connected to everyone around us by the breath we all share. We begin to understand that life is a classroom, in which we are all here to learn. Ultimately, nobody fails the curriculum, which is to learn to love unconditionally.

When the heart is balanced, we come to recognize that we are not defective creatures unworthy of love but rather precious children of the Universe. We begin to love ourselves in a deeply compassionate and unconditional way, which opens the door for us to extend such love outward. Because the heart rules balance, it can remain open and flowing only if we are willing to receive the good we give out. In order to be balanced, love must flow both ways.

One of my favorite Chinese sayings is "Until you are willing to receive what you give, and willing to give what you receive, you do not understand love." This is what the heart center is about: learning to balance the act of giving and receiving love without restriction or ulterior motives.

The balanced heart awakens our capacity to accept love from others. It ushers in relief because nothing heals more profoundly than to feel lovable and to be loved in spite of our weaknesses. In fact, many metaphysicians, myself included, believe that the root of all emotional and even physical illness originates with the feeling of a loss of love, more specifically a belief that we are undeserving of love. When the heart is balanced and love flows, emotional wounds begin to heal. We also begin to break free of the negative patterns of behavior that keep us feeling defensive and judgmental, isolated and alone, unable to reach out or to ask for or accept help.

Love, as opposed to sensuality or sexuality, is a quiet and contemplative energy. This energy, originating in our spiritual heart, flows through our physical heart and radiates outward. It is the most compelling energy there is, both to the sender and to the recipients. It is an uplifting, calming, reassuring vibration that eases even those who have been most traumatized. Remember the last time you were in love? Remember the exhilarating and deeply nurturing feeling it brought to you? When the heart is operating at its best, every day feels like being in love.

A HEART-BASED PERSON

When your heart is balanced, you accept yourself and others without judgment. You look for the beauty and Divine Spirit in everyone and overlook their weaknesses. You are kind and forgiving, slow to find fault, and quick to pardon. An open heart is tolerant and optimistic, resourceful and humorous. Your intentions are kind, and your generosity is genuine. A person with a balanced heart is very healing and comforting to be around, because you feel safe and make those around you feel accepted and appreciated without condition. Your perspective is always oriented toward solutions rather than problems, and your expectations for positive outcomes are very high. You tend to attract the good things in life to you, and you may be perceived by others as "lucky" or "blessed."

It's not hard to identify people with a balanced heart. They are easy-going, accepting, graceful, and soothing to be around. They have a charismatic quality about them, drawing others like a warm and healing fire. A person with a balanced heart seems to bring oxygen into a room. Everyone around such a person seems to be able to breathe more deeply and easily. A balanced heart stirs up happiness and laughter and a sense of safety. When you encounter such a loving presence, you feel more loving and lovable yourself. You can particularly feel it in the chest area, as your anxiety fades, constrictions ease up, and positive energy fills your body.

I had a client named Maureen who was just such a person. Around fifty years old, she was plain in appearance, short, thirty pounds or so overweight, and unfashionably dressed. There was no reason you'd give her a second glance—except for the glow around her, which made it difficult to take your eyes off her. She was radiant! Maureen worked at a dry cleaner two days a week, but her real work was taking care of AIDS babies, wards of the state who at that time were certain to die. Her devotion and boundless generosity in caring for these little castoffs was breathtaking. She had two or three babies at any given time and provided them all with unconditional love and acceptance. The amazing thing was that in spite of the stress related to this work, Maureen was endlessly cheerful and genuinely grateful for every single blessing God had given her. She was grateful for the sun. She was grateful for the rain. She saw a silver lining in every circumstance and never complained about anything. She was always quick with a joke and had time to listen to everyone. In other words, she was an angel on Earth. Her balanced heart was wide open, and being in her presence always managed to open mine a little wider, too. Every time I spoke with Maureen, her vibration lifted my heart and left me feeling as though I, too, had just received a healing.

People like Maureen are gifts to us all. I believe God plants these secret angels in our lives to help us remember to focus on what is most important, which is giving and receiving love. In connecting to them, we reconnect to our own heart and Higher Self. That is the power of an open heart chakra. As the saying goes, "All the world loves a lover." It's true. A person who generates love from the heart is the most attractive person you will ever meet.

Have you ever known a heart-based person?

_____

Have you ever committed your heart to a cause or person in need?

_____

_____

THE PROTECTIVE HEART

Unfortunately, life being what it is, we will inevitably face situations that create fear and cause pain. To protect ourselves from this pain, we engage what is called, in esoteric terms, the "protective heart." This is the energetic covering over the heart center that blocks out painful experiences. This covering can be activated at will, and it often is, especially when we are young and extremely vulnerable. Unfortunately, the protective heart has no power to discriminate, and once it covers our heart, it filters out everything. Like a total eclipse, it cuts us off from all feeling and sentiment, good and bad.

The heart's protective covering protects us from the agony of heartbreak, and it is helpful in a crisis, allowing us to continue on in spite of our pain. But it is intended as a temporary shield; when we pull this protective cover over our hearts as a permanent way of life, we become distanced and cut ourselves off from others.

I had a close friend, Mike, whose mother died unexpectedly after a short illness when he was only ten years old. Unaware that she was even sick, he was surprised when he came home from school one day and found her gone. When he asked where she was, his father and aunts lied to him, saying she was on a trip and would be coming home soon. When funeral arrangements were under way and he suddenly realized she would never come home again, he was confused and devastated. Not being told the truth may have been an attempt to protect him, but it didn't. It made his loss infinitely worse, because not only did he lose his mom, he also lost confidence in his father and aunts as well; in a way, he lost his entire family. As a way to punish everyone for his pain, he decided that he would never again show his true feelings. He wouldn't even cry at his mother's funeral, and he didn't.

The moment Mike made that decision, he pulled his protective heart covering firmly into place. Doing so helped him cope with his over-whelming losses at the time, but unfortunately he never lifted it after-ward. Blocked in his inability to open his heart, he was unable to intimately connect with anyone. It was as if there were a thick padding wrapped around his heart that prevented anyone from getting too close. As an adult, his girlfriends found this extremely frustrating, and after a while they left him. He wasn't malicious, just emotionally unavailable and withholding due to his unhealed past trauma. Mike never under-stood why his girlfriends left him, even when they told him that he was cold and aloof. He didn't feel he was. But with his protective heart chakra in place, they weren't able to feel his warmth. And because he didn't know that warmth himself, he didn't know what was missing. Yet his intuition told him there was truth to what they said. After many breakups and two divorces, Mike was finally willing to look at himself, and thus began the adventure of opening his heart. It took the help of a talented spiritual counselor, many workshops and books, and a very insistent yet patient third wife, not to mention his own loneliness, to con-vince him to finally remove his protective heart covering.

This happened spontaneously one day while he was out in the garden with his wife, planting daffodils and tulips. As his wife handed him another bulb to place in the ground, he was suddenly struck by the realization of how deeply he loved her and how much he wanted her to know this. Rather than dive back into the safety of his isolation, he allowed his feelings to flood through him, and in a split second his heart center burst wide open. He felt as though someone had flung back the curtains and let in the light. All the years of grief and sadness that he had carried around melted away in a moment, exposing his sweet and fragile self. In his vulnerability, he finally connected with his wife, the garden, the ground, the bulbs, his life. He felt able to breathe in fully for the first time since he was a child. The feeling was so marvelous, so life affirming, he could hardly bear it. The loneliness lifted, and so did the fear. Like a soothing balm washing away years of sadness, grief, and isolation, his tears began to flow and wouldn't stop. His heart eased open more and more, and with a deep and cleansing breath, he stepped into life. Intuitively his wife understood what was happening to him. They didn't say a word. No words were necessary. They just held each other and cried.

What events or experiences have caused you to engage your protective heart?

_____

_____

_____

Is your protective heart still in place?

_____

_____

_____

What attempts have you made to remove your guard and open your heart once again?

_____

_____

Have you succeeded? How does your heart feel now?

_____

_____

A CLOSED HEART CHAKRA

If your spiritual heart is off balance or shut down, you have a tendency to withdraw from intimacy and personal closeness. You may also be extremely withholding and intentionally push people away. When the heart is closed, the world cannot enter, and you become isolated and disconnected from your sources of nurturing. In such an energetic paralysis, everything feels threatening, even dangerous, causing you to become extremely cautious and on guard. Because you will feel no connection or kinship with others, you may become critical, suspicious, and defensive, which only exacerbates your problem. Having a closed heart sets you up for rejection. Because of your inaccessibility, people feel unsafe around you and naturally put up defenses of their own. You may even be paranoid and perceive the world as against you.

Almost every person with a closed heart chakra is actually frightened and wounded. They try to hide their injuries and cover up their vulnerabilities with a harsh or steely facade. Their closed heart sets up vicious cycle after vicious cycle, where their fear of being rejected causes them to push others away. This then leads them to being rejected and to pushing people away even more. It's similar to a wounded animal. When injured, a normally loving and peaceful animal turns vicious because it is in pain and afraid of further injury. When our hearts become injured, we can become just as violent and defensive as animals do, if not more.

If your heart shuts down completely, you may be inclined toward secrecy, scheming, defensiveness, sabotage, and betrayal. Addictions, particularly to alcohol and drugs, will immediately cut you off from your heart and shut down your capacity to be aware of either your own or anyone else's feelings. A closed heart chakra is usually the result of childhood abuses, excessive materialism, emotional abandonment, betrayal, family breakdown, drug, alcohol, or other addiction, or mental illness. Needless to say, closed heart chakras are in epidemic proportion worldwide and are the cause of our greatest injuries to one another. You can tell if a person has a closed heart chakra by how genuine and self-revealing they are. If they seem superficial or act false in any way, you know that their heart is shut down.

People with a closed heart are challenging to be around. They feel unsafe, and because of their absorption with their own pain, they are usually insensitive to those around them. Yet because we all to some degree come from wounded backgrounds, and because those who inflicted our wounds themselves had closed hearts, our contacts with other closed hearts bring our old psychic injuries to the surface once again. Therefore, the presence of one person with a powerfully closed heart chakra has a negative domino effect, throwing everyone who has contact with him or her into some form of doubt and bringing out the worst in everyone. Entire countries have gone to war because of the domino effect of a closed heart.

The truth is, of course, that people with a closed heart chakra are emotionally wounded. Their only tool for protecting themselves is emotional unavailability. They are just as lovable as anyone else underneath it all, but they are harder to connect with because they make it all so difficult.

The most famous story of the closed heart chakra is Charles Dickens's tale of Scrooge, the miser in *A Christmas Carol*. I think there's a Scrooge in all of us at times, because we all have moments when we want everyone else to feel as bad as we do so we won't feel alone. If you know someone, or are someone, with a closed heart chakra, you need more than anything else to be loving and accepting. If any one of us is hurting, on some unconscious collective level, we are all hurting.

HOW OPEN IS YOUR HEART?

	Yes	No	Sometimes
I am lighthearted.	_____	_____	_____
I allow people in.	_____	_____	_____
I naturally trust others.	_____	_____	_____
I enjoy helping others.	_____	_____	_____
I am quick to forgive.	_____	_____	_____
I don't take offense easily.	_____	_____	_____
I am naturally patient.	_____	_____	_____
I feel good about who I am.	_____	_____	_____
I spend my time doing what I love.	_____	_____	_____
I can turn any situation into a pleasant experience.	_____	_____	_____
I laugh easily and a lot.	_____	_____	_____
I have confidence that my heart's desire will come.	_____	_____	_____
I have fond memories of my past.	_____	_____	_____
I am generous and like giving cards and gifts.	_____	_____	_____
I take good care of myself and treat myself well.	_____	_____	_____

If you answered no to any one of these statements, your heart is somewhat closed. If you answered no to two or three statements, you are slightly imbalanced and should follow the suggestions for slight imbalances at the end of the chapter. If you answered no to four to seven statements, then your heart is moderately closed and you should follow the suggestions for adjusting moderate imbalances. If you answered no to eight or more statements, then your heart is seriously shut down. You should follow the suggestions for serious imbalances in order to heal your heart and engage in life more.

EXCLUSIVITY

One symptom of an imbalanced spiritual heart is the tendency to feel exclusive, superior, or in some way better than other human beings. Such imbalance is apparent in racism, religious righteousness, and ethnic divisions, to name a few examples. You might be certain that this would never describe you, and yet in a million subtle ways, we all fall victim to this, closing our hearts, indulging our egos, and distancing ourselves from others, believing we are in our own special way above the rest. For example, have you ever felt a twinge of scorn toward a beggar on the street, disdaining him for not working? Or a "welfare mother" for having "too many kids"? Have you ever considered yourself "a cut above the rest" because you have a master's degree or graduated from a certain school, or work in a certain job? At one point in my own life, I felt a smug degree of superiority simply because I was a flight attendant for TWA as opposed to American Airlines (which was said with a sneer), because our uniforms were "more professional." As ridiculous as it was, I thought I was a better person than my American flight attendant peers because I considered my uniform better looking!

How absurd! Yet we are all guilty of such foolishness. Whether we establish our superiority by the car we drive, the house we live in, the kind of clothes we wear, or any other superficial factor, the truth is we do this, and we do it a lot! Yet we are hurting ourselves when we do it because such elitism isolates our heart and disrupts our ability to receive the flow of love from the Universe. Separating ourselves from others reveals more about how we feel about ourselves than about how we feel about others. Fear drives this separating behavior. We do it when we feel insecure and secretly doubt our own worthiness of love. We then attempt to elevate our low self-esteem by diminishing others. The more we do it, the more we hurt ourselves. Though it may temporarily distract us from the pain of self-rejection that we are feeling inside, the distraction doesn't last.

The more we distance ourselves, the more unworthy we secretly feel we are, setting up a vicious cycle. The way to rebalance the heart is to stop establishing differences between "us" and "them" and notice where we are all alike.

I had a client, Laurie, who was a real prima donna—a "Jewish American princess," as she herself put it. The only daughter of wealthy real estate brokers in Chicago, she had a terribly condescending attitude toward most people, especially men. She was even more disdainful of men who weren't Jewish. Not surprisingly, her love life suffered greatly.

We talked frequently about her attitude and how it harmed her emotionally, but Laurie just couldn't seem to change her beliefs. She really did believe she was special! Imagine her surprise when, quite unexpectedly, she became attracted to her new neighbor, a man named Donald, who happened to be a middle-class Irish Catholic schoolteacher. According to her standards, he was a completely unacceptable partner because he wasn't "rich enough, educated enough, and God forbid, he isn't Jewish!" Nevertheless, the attraction was so strong that they began to date anyway. They hit it off famously, and within four months, Donald spontaneously proposed. Not expecting this, all of her prejudices suddenly hit her right between the eyes. She couldn't find a single reason to say no except for her discriminating attitude.

"This is a complete disaster!" she told me. "It's a very bad joke on God's part. I'll never be able to marry him," she went on, although she obviously wanted to.

"Why not?" I asked.

"Because he isn't good enough for me!" she confessed. "I want someone with money, a nice car, and a Harvard education, and someone who is Jewish!" she exclaimed. "I know it's wrong, but I need someone like me, with class and status. I know it'll never work!"

"But you said yourself that you really love him."

"Yes, but that's not enough!"

"What exactly are you afraid of?" I pressed further.

"My friends! My family! They'll think I married beneath me!" she cried. "How embarrassing!"

"And you? What do you think?"

"I think when he finds out what they think, and what superficial people we all are, he won't love me anymore!"

"So, Laurie, you fear that if he knows you really well, and gets to know your friends and family, and how prejudiced and judgmental you all can be, he won't love you. Is that right?"

"Yes," she said. "I think that's what I really fear, now that I think about it."

"Laurie, real love is naturally faithful and tenacious," I replied. "I think it won't matter. I think Donald's genuine love for you and yours for him will override everyone's preconceived notions and soften everyone's biased view, yours included. Follow your heart on this one, not your fears."

In meeting and falling in love with Donald, the Universe threw Laurie a curveball. In falling in love with someone she would otherwise dismiss as inferior, she was offered the opportunity to experience real love and not some prepackaged idea of love. It also gave her the chance to leave her mental castle behind and join the rest of the human race. Happily, in Laurie's case, she did follow her heart, changed her attitude, and married him. Nine years and two kids later, Laurie and Donald remain very married. And Donald is her parents' favorite son-in-law. It turned out Laurie's fears were more her problem than anyone else's. When she dropped her superiority complex, she allowed herself to receive a sustained and loving partner, albeit in a package she never expected. Together, Laurie and Donald now lead workshops on interfaith marriage and find it spiritually rewarding to share their experiences with others who are in the same challenging boat.

What distinctions do you secretly harbor that separate you from others?

_____

_____

What discriminating attitudes were prevalent in your home when you were growing up?

_____

_____

What areas of your life bring out your superiority complexes?

_____

_____

What areas of your life bring out your inferiority complexes?

_____

_____

Think of someone you feel superior or inferior to. Write down all the things you can think of that you have in common.

_____

_____

_____

AN OVERLY EMPATHIC HEART

Just as a closed heart causes problems, so does one that is too wide open. Such a heart causes people to be overly sensitive to the energy of those around them, so much so that they actually absorb other people's energy. This can be psychically and physically draining, especially when the energy is dissonant or angry. When you are overly empathic, the resonance you feel with others is nonselective. If someone is happy, you feel happy. If someone is miserable, you feel miserable. You are at the mercy of feeling whatever anyone else is feeling, whether you want to or not. It's as if you were a lightning rod in an electrical storm. If energy is being discharged, you attract it.

Being an intuitive, this was my problem for many years. When I did a reading for a joyful or peaceful person, it was a great pleasure, but when I read for someone who was angry, scared, or in pain, I found myself swimming in the very same sea—and drowning. It took me years of study with my spiritual teachers to learn not to absorb the energy of others and instead to stay in my own heart. What I had to learn was the difference between love and sentimentality. Sentimentality, I discovered, is being a member of the soft-focus, slow-motion "woulda, shoulda, coulda" club of life, where we want everything to be pleasant, smooth, and calm. Sentimentality wants to whitewash life and doesn't respect the passion and pain that go along with growth. With love, on the other hand, we can honor and support someone without interference or judgment. We can resist the urge to rescue them, no matter how difficult it is to watch their choices unfold. When I fall into sentimental rapport with someone, I want him to feel better right away. But to be honest about it, this isn't for his benefit as much as it is for my own, since I don't want to feel his pain.

Though we may tell ourselves that absorbing another's hurt is kind and loving, in fact it is really an attempt to relieve our own discomfort. If we are loving, we realize that all of life's experiences, even the painful ones, need to be honored, and that we need to stay in our own energy field. We must not try to control outcomes or assume we even have a right to get involved. We all need our experiences in order to learn. If we attempt to tamper with those of others, even with the best of intentions, we may be setting them back on their path.

Though being an empath can feel like being a turtle without a shell, vulnerable and exposed to the elements, you need not suffer through others' energetic storms. They can actually make you sick. I had a client named Ramon, a natural healer, who was an acutely sensitive and loving person. He experienced great physical anxiety every time he was exposed to anyone's pain, sadness, or discomfort. It didn't matter whether these emotions were coming from the teller at the bank, the irritable clerk at the grocery store, or his passionate and at times volatile girlfriend. Ramon was so sensitive to these energies that they sent shock waves through his nervous system—so much so, in fact, that he developed a severe case of eczema. He tried everything under the sun to relieve this condition, but because he couldn't detach his heart from those around him, his eczema persisted. Once he understood the psychic dynamic of his condition, he realized that in addition to receiving therapies such as hypnosis, meditation, and conventional medical treatments, he had to also intentionally detach from the vibrations of others if he wanted to heal. Eventually, with much discipline and awareness, he began to improve. He asked me one day, exasperated with the intense reactions he continued to have around certain people, "Sonia, I understand that I am not to interfere with others' lessons, but how do I stop feeling their frustration, especially when it belongs to someone I live with, like my girlfriend? It is still almost impossible for me to filter out her energy, and it drains me."

I gave him the same advice my teachers gave me when I first began to do psychic readings and would feel overwhelmed: "Whenever you feel as though you are absorbing someone else's energy, you can always use your left and right feet and leave. Walk away from them, and send them blessings and prayers on the way out. This will help you disengage from the field and not interfere with their process, all the while that you are being loving."

The answer seemed so obvious to him that he laughed out loud. "Of course," he said. "Why not?" I agreed. "Give your sensitive self a break. Let it be that easy." We don't have to make everything as painful as we do. It is a slow recovery, but Ramon is gradually getting his energy field under control and his heart chakra balanced. He also got a pair of running shoes to use when all else fails. Slowly his skin is healing.

HOW EMPATHIC ARE YOU?

Do other people's moods affect you physically? Is this true with everyone or just certain people? In what way?

_____

_____

When you are exposed to negative energy, what do you do?

_____

_____

Are you aware of changes in your mood when you are around certain people and/or places?

_____

What situations or people affect you the most? What catches you off guard?

_____

_____

TRY THIS!

A Balancing Bath

One way to clear your aura of other people's vibrations and come back to balance is to take an Epsom salt bath. Buy a quart of Epsom salt, fill a tub with lukewarm water, and pour the entire contents into the bath. It helps to add a few drops of essential oil (preferably rose oil, which calms and balances the heart) and to soak in the tub for at least twenty minutes. Because Epsom salt is very drying to the skin, you will want to follow it with a brisk shower. This cleansing does wonders for psychic overload. (In case you find Epsom salt too drying, use baking soda. It works equally well.)

POWER OF ATTRACTION

When the heart is open and balanced, we enter into a state of attraction to what we need, because the power of love is magnetic and harmonious. If our hearts are open, we find ourselves attracting all sorts of positive experiences. As if by magic, these expressions often correspond to our exact needs at the time. This is often called synchronicity, or "being at the right place at the right time." I call it resonance, which means "like attracts like."

For example, I had a client named Don, a part-time taxicab driver from Chile, who had attended one of my workshops. He was having a terrible time; he was struggling to make ends meet, and had no love life whatsoever, and because he was under such stress, he was floundering in school. He was desperate for a change and thought maybe I could help.

As he learned about the chakras and how they work, he was particularly drawn to the idea of opening his heart chakra as a way of pulling in more positive experiences. "I need to do something," he said. "I'm broke, scared to death of blowing it in school, and feeling very lonely. Maybe opening my heart will change my luck. It can't hurt. Things can't get much worse than they are now."

And so he began greeting everyone who entered his cab with a warm smile and genuine enthusiasm. He listened empathetically when they spoke to him, even if they were cursing and yelling. He drove carefully, he kept his taxi clean, and he was friendly—three very unusual qualities in a Chicago taxicab driver.

Practicing his new open-hearted attitude, things began to change in the very first month. "It was amazing!" he said. "As if by magic, the minute I'd drop someone off, someone else would be right there, waiting for a ride, as if waiting for me. I was never without a fare, whereas before, sometimes I would drive around up to half an hour between passengers. I also received more than two thousand dollars in tips, the largest being a hundred-dollar bill given to me by a woman who was late for a real estate closing. I picked her up in a downpour, when there wasn't a taxi to be found anywhere. I was also offered a job driving a private limousine for another passenger who apparently owns a string of nightclubs in town. He really likes me. I'm interviewing with him after finals. Because I started to make money, I was able to go home a little earlier than usual, and I could study for my classes. That took a tremendous amount of pressure off me. The best part was, however, that while taking this beautiful woman to O'Hare Airport in a blizzard, we struck up a conversation and discovered that we both were studying immigration law. Can you believe she asked me out? She actually called me when she returned to Chicago ten days later. We met for coffee and hit it off immediately. I don't know if it'll go anywhere, but it did wonders for my ego. I asked her if she had ever invited a taxi driver out on a date before. She said, 'No, never. But you seemed so open and safe, I thought I'd take a chance.'"

Don's experiences weren't simply coincidence or luck. They were a demonstration of the magnetic power of an open heart chakra. We are all unconsciously in search of love. Whenever we feel its presence in our environment, we can't help but be drawn to it. There is no more compelling energy in the world. When a person acts lovingly, he or she becomes irresistible.

What do you want to attract in your life?

_____

_____

How successful have you been in attracting things into your life in the past?

_____

_____

How lovingly can you imagine your heart's desire?

_____

_____

LOVE IS EVERY MAN FOR HIMSELF

One of the greatest myths in the realm of love is the belief that when we fall in love with someone, we can expect to live together "happily ever after." This misconception is not surprising, since we have all grown up with fairy tales that suggest that merely finding a beloved will solve our problems. How many times has it been suggested that if only we met the right one, he or she would fill our void and make us feel happy and secure and loved? I know that in my own life, this was the inferred plan from the time the doctor slapped my bottom and said, "It's a girl!"

For so many of us, love is really nothing more than a disguised demand: "You take care of me now, and you better do it better than Mommy and Daddy did." This unrealistic demand is the basis of all relationship nightmares and heartbreaks. As long as we think love means another person makes us feel good, we will continue to miss the wonder of real love; we will remain miserable, frustrated, and disappointed. Sadly, the truth is that no one can fill our voids. At best we can enter into agreements with one another to be companions and friends as we learn to fulfill ourselves. Real love is not a promise to be rescued from our demons. In fact, real love is not about us at all. It is instead the decision to care for another as much as we care for ourselves and to accept him or her for who they are, without condition, exception, or judgment. This is a very tall order to fulfill, and it is nearly impossible to do so until we accept that we alone are responsible for our happiness. We cannot cling to another person, even when this is disguised as "love."

We are able to love only when we are able to not attach, control, or manipulate the other in an attempt to make ourselves feel secure. We must be willing to stand on our own two feet. In other words, we must be able to love ourselves, fully, faithfully, and without condition. We can certainly help one another grow, but others can't and won't do the work of our growth for us. Whenever a relationship contains clinging dependencies that pose as love, one or the other partner will rebel, and the relationship will reel into chaos. Interestingly, no one seems to be able to escape this lesson, as it is necessary for our own spiritual happiness and for the evolution of the planet. Indeed, it is what we have come to Earth to learn.

The reality is that after we fall in love with someone, after the romance wears off, the real work of love begins. I had a client, Lenore, who was married for thirty-five years to a very wealthy doctor, whom she had partnered since they were teenagers. She worked very hard at small jobs while Rob went to school, learned his vocation, and ultimately made a fortune. Then she stayed home, raised their three children, and focused exclusively on "being a good wife." Just when she expected to enter into "happily-ever-after land," Rob had an affair and simultaneously lost a small fortune. When she came to me, devastated, she couldn't utter a single sentence without blaming him for ruining her life. She vacillated between hating him and fearing he would divorce her for the other woman. Mostly she wondered how, if that were to happen, she would ever pay her bills and assume responsibility for herself.

Fully expecting me to join in her diatribe against him, Lenore was stunned when I suggested that it was her call from the Universe to learn to love. She said, "What do you mean? I've loved him all my life! I've done everything for him! He owes me!"

"That's just it. Everything you did was with the ulterior expectation that he would assume responsibility for you. In serving him, you were really serving your secret fears about being unable to support yourself and take care of your needs. He instinctively felt this. His digressions are really opportunities to encourage you to let go of him, let go of your fears, and get a life that fulfills you in a more honest way than pleasing him out of fear has provided. In a strange and convoluted way, his behavior is loving, because on the soul level, he knows there is more to you than what you are settling for."

This was a viewpoint she hadn't expected, and yet when she heard it voiced out loud, she admitted, "You're right! It has been a long time since I've actually felt love for him. I've stayed in this relationship because of the money, comfort, and predictability it affords. I do feel my own life is undeveloped, and if I were to be honest, that is what I'm most angry about. If he divorces me, then she gets all the goods, and I end up on the street!"

I suggested that rather than continuing to focus on him or his girlfriend, Lenore focus instead on her unlived life. Though she could argue a case against him until the cows came home, it wouldn't help her heal. "Start by going back to school and developing your talents," I suggested. "When you had your children, you abandoned your writing ambitions. You have real talent there. Then get a life and get some friends. Stop depending upon Rob to be your entertainment committee. Step on your own two feet, and carve a path of your own."

"Though I know this is right, I have to admit that it feels overwhelming, and I'm afraid," she confessed. "Doesn't that sound pitiful?"

"No, not really," I replied. "You've lived a cloistered existence all these years, so you are a novice at independence. To make it easier, begin at the beginning." I encouraged her to work at the local bookstore as a way of reentering the world, and to sign up for a writing class two days a week as well.

"What about divorcing Rob? What about the other woman?" she persisted.

"Ignore that for now. Adopt an 'every man for himself' attitude, but don't declare war. And don't do things to spite him. Do them because they're the right thing to do. And then see what happens."

Relieved to have some direction and not really wanting a divorce, she took my advice and got a job that very week. She loved her writing class so much that she signed up for another course in creative writing at the local university. Involved in her own experiences, she actually found herself forgetting about Rob during the day—no small feat, considering that she had been obsessed with him when she came to see me. Because she was having so much fun in her newly discovered life, she was kinder and more pleasant to Rob when she did see him. He became intrigued with her because she wasn't as available and because he no longer seemed to carry the burden of being her life. He, in turn, had to learn to cook for himself and do his own laundry; he even had to talk to his own children, because she was no longer there to do it for him!

They knew things were turning around, when one day quite spontaneously, as they were putting away the breakfast dishes, Rob said something silly, and they both burst out laughing and couldn't stop. The more they laughed, the more they wanted to laugh, and in those few moments their defenses dropped and their hearts burst wide open. As if waking up from a bad dream, they caught each other's eye and knew everything would be all right. It was a steep learning curve for them, but as each of them took responsibility for meeting his or her own needs, the capacity to really love the other opened up. Rob became more appreciative of Lenore when they were together; she no longer perceived him as "Dad" with the paycheck. The girlfriend mysteriously disappeared. Bit by bit, they were able to recapture the love they had felt when they first married.

In what areas of your life do you feel resentful?

_____

_____

What would you love to do that you are not doing?

_____

_____

What secret expectations do you place on others for your well-being?

_____

_____

In what areas are you willing to forgive, forget, and assume more responsibility for your personal happiness?

_____

_____

In what areas are you willing to become more independent?

_____

_____

When have you last laughed with your partner?

_____

_____

FORGIVENESS BALANCES THE HEART

If emotional wounding closes the heart, forgiveness opens it. It is all too easy to build a shrine to our broken hearts and settle for the emptiness of resentment, instead of finding the courage to go beyond our pain. The only way to achieve the blessings of love is to be willing to let go and forgive. In forgiveness, we end the separations that cause us to feel unlovable and hurt. We reclaim the truth that no one can keep us from feeling love and being loved. Forgiveness takes a second look at our history with a compassionate eye. It frees us from our past, honors our lessons, and gives us the opportunity to become the healer instead of the wounded one.

Jerry, handsome and charming on the surface, was a wounded and angry man inside, having suffered a painful childhood marked by alcoholism, emotional neglect, and physical abuse. He kept it well hidden, however—or so he thought. It wasn't until his fourteenth year of marriage that his life fell apart. First, his wife asked for a separation; then his parents turned the family business over to his brother without telling him. These two events sent shock waves through his system, and he found his life in a scrambled mess. He knew that he had held resentments toward his family. As a child, being the oldest of twelve, he had felt burdened with unfair responsibilities. His father was always away working or at the local bar drinking with his friends. His mom, overwhelmed with her life, had a short fuse and a long switch; she expected the children to keep everything under control—a near-impossible task for any child.

At eighteen, after a big argument with his father, Jerry left home. He was intent on doing things his way, but he secretly felt banished as a failure. These childhood experiences left him bitter, angry, and resentful and made all his later relationships impossible. As a way of coping with his wounded heart, he drank to keep people away. This only made him feel angrier and even more unlovable, setting up a vicious cycle of depression, insecurity, and rage. Finally, with his separation from his wife and the betrayal of his family, he hit bottom. He had to seek help.

Jerry contacted a trusted friend who suggested that he enroll in a healing workshop as a way to work out some of his rage and hurt. At one point in the workshop, he was asked to imagine that his parents were dying and what he felt. When he did this, he more than imagined the scene. He actually had a vision of his parents gravely injured in the hospital, every bone broken, in great pain and fighting for life. Seeing them so vulnerable, he instantly remembered every loving gesture they had ever made toward him. He realized that they had done their best all along and that that's all they or anyone else could do. The vision of their deaths was so horrifying that his heart instantly flooded with love and compassion for his mother and father. He realized just how important they were to him and how his bitterness was ruining his life. He was perceiving them as against him, when in fact it was he who was pushing them away. Only his changes, not theirs, would relieve him of his misery. In that moment, he decided that he had to let go of his resentments and forgive them before it was too late.

After the workshop, he went directly to their home and told them he loved them completely and that he forgave them for everything in the past. His father, taken aback by his open heart, cried and held him closely. His mother, always more cautious, attempted to keep her distance, but eventually she couldn't resist his love and responded as well. The minute he forgave them, an incredible burden lifted off his chest. As he drove back home, he felt the same love and compassion for himself. He no longer felt isolated or unworthy, and his own tears began to flow. He relaxed.

Two days later, when he was out for a run, he decided to talk to God. "I'm tired of missing your cues, God!" he yelled into the Universe. "Turn up the volume so I can hear you!" When he returned home, he received a call. His parents had been in a terrible car accident. They were gravely injured and weren't expected to live. Stunned by the fact that his premonition had come true, he was profoundly grateful that his last conversation with them had been one of love and forgiveness. Knowing that his parents knew how much he loved and appreciated them somehow made the tragedy easier to bear. Apparently God had heard him that morning. The message was loud and clear.

Who are you angry with and holding resentments toward?

_____

_____

What are you most angry about?

_____

_____

How long has it been since you last communicated with those you resent?

_____

_____

In what way are you responsible for your part of the separation?

_____

_____

What can you learn from your anger?

_____

Can you/are you willing to forgive?

_____

What gift can you find in your relationship? _____

_____

☀ TRY THIS!

A Happy Heart Party

When you succeed in opening your heart, it is cause for celebration. Throw yourself a "happy heart party," and invite everyone you love. Ask each guest to bring a meaningful gift, something that soothes their own soul. It can be a cherished CD or book, a bottle of their favorite bath oil, or even a video of their favorite movie. Once everyone arrives, first open two or three bottles of inexpensive champagne, pour them into a bucket or tub, and have everyone wash their feet in it, to symbolize cleansing away the dust from the past. Then go into the kitchen and bake heart-shaped cookies and decorate them with every kind of sparkly decoration you can find. While they are baking, make a grab bag and place all the gifts inside. Then let everyone have a turn reaching in for a gift. Finish the party by eating your cookies and acknowledging each other for your shared friendship and support.

LOVE IS THE SMALL THINGS

As we awaken to love, we sometimes feel we must now perform extraordinary acts to prove to others and ourselves that we are indeed loving. Unfortunately, even the best intentions can go awry because ordinary life doesn't always appreciate them. Besides, needing to be extraordinary in any way is still your ego talking and not your heart. It is much more useful to forget about extraordinary gestures of love and simply love extraordinarily in the daily gestures of life. When serving breakfast to your kids, for example, be a little more patient and smile instead of tossing their cereal in front of them with a sharp "Hurry up or you'll be late!" When you open the morning paper, ask your spouse, "What section would you like to read first this morning?" and then hand it over. In other words, every ordinary moment throughout the day affords you an opportunity to be loving. It isn't so much what you do that demonstrates love as the way in which you do it.

When I was a teenager, I often called my father late in the evening to come and get me because I didn't have a car. He showed up every time, and more importantly, he came lovingly. He never made me feel guilty or even made a big deal about it. He just quietly showed up. His acts of love were founded in his consistency. I had the benefit of knowing I could count on him, which laid a foundation of security under my feet. My mother had her own way of turning the small matters of life into opportunities to love as well. Whenever I needed a costume, a dress, or something special to wear, she would stop everything and get to work. Not only did she sew for me, she did it with enthusiasm! The best way to usher love into your life is to do what you must but do it lovingly. And if you must do something that you don't want to, use it as an opportunity to practice love.

When I first became a flight attendant, I found that I wasn't particularly good at it, because I didn't like to serve people over and over again. In fact, I resented it, which made my job unbearable. I called my teacher Charlie one day and said, "I hate this job. I am destined to be greater than this!" He laughed at me and asked, "Greater than what?"

"Greater than serving coffee, tea, and bad food all day to cranky passengers. I want to be an intuitive and a healer, not a flight attendant!"

Charlie was silent for a moment, and then he said, "Until you serve everyone you encounter with love in your heart, you are not worthy or capable of helping anyone. Every passenger on board is your teacher. You are arrogant in distancing yourself from them. Each one of those passengers holds the spirit of God within them, and until you see that, you don't see anything that would qualify you as an intuitive or a healer. Now go back to work and quit your complaining. Be grateful to those passengers. The more unpleasant they are, the more they are helping you learn to love!"

That was a slap in the face for me. And yet he was right. I had a bad attitude, and it was making me, and everyone I was in contact with, miserable. I decided that day to change my attitude and do my job with love. Overnight the job transformed. I began to enjoy the people and have more fun. I even got better trips, which was a miracle because my job was seniority based and I was near the bottom of that totem pole. The real surprise came when I was asked to do the first-class service from Chicago to London every weekend for a year. This was like getting a paid vacation once a week, and it was probably one of the best years in my life. When I did my work with love, no matter what work it was, life became a joy.

This is the secret to opening your heart. When you make the generous decision to surrender your ego and participate fully in your life, without withholding, without separating yourself, without needing to be special, without wanting something special in return, life bursts wide open and brings you every possible gift you can imagine and more. Life lived lovingly restores balance and attracts grace. And it's easy, once you decide that you want this in your life. Mother Teresa summed it up best when she said, "I do not do great things. I only do small things with great love."

In what way can you be more loving:

to your partner?

to your children?

_____

to your parents?

_____

to your boss?

_____

to your neighbor?

_____

to the irritating customer at work?

_____

to your whiny friend?

_____

In my work as an intuitive counselor for over thirty years, I have come to realize that even though appearances lead us to believe that we are different from one another, the truth is that we are really very much alike. We all have the same concerns, the same needs, and the same fears. Our heart chakra spins out of balance when we neglect to provide ourselves with what we need in order to remain nurtured and nurturing. The best remedies for a balanced heart are the sweet and soul-nurturing activities that leave us feeling cared for, connected to others, and receptive to all the blessings of the Universe.

AWAKENING YOUR HEART

When your heart is *slightly* imbalanced

- Offer to help the new person at work.

- Read poetry.

- Hold hands with the people you love.

- Give someone a bear hug.

- Invite someone over for dinner or make someone dinner and deliver it to their home.

- Buy a dozen postcards, go to your favorite coffee shop, and write them out to your friends and family.

- Think of your best qualities while soaking in a warm bath with a few drops of rose essential oil to open the heart chakra.

- Carry your baby picture in your wallet, and look at it whenever you are feeling unloved.

- Write a letter of appreciation to someone who has made a positive difference in your life.

- Rent a love-story movie.

- Eat fresh green vegetables and salads.

- Wear something green to open and balance the heart chakra.

When your heart is *moderately* imbalanced

- Apologize to those you have hurt.

- Spend a weekend in nature.

- Say "I'd love to" when someone makes a request.

- Make a gratitude scrapbook.

- Surprise someone with a long-distance phone card as a gift.

- Offer to baby-sit free your best friend's or neighbor's children.

- Go to a reputable intuitive or healer, and have them give you an intuitive reading or do some energy work on you.

- Make a photo collage of all the people you love, and display it prominently in your home.

- Send an anonymous care basket or flowers to someone who is feeling blue.

- Rent the movie *Moonstruck* by Norman Jewison or *How the Grinch Stole Christmas* by Chuck Jones.

- Write poetry, and share it with others.

- Read a funny book.

- Have a loving chat with a childhood best friend.

When your heart is *profoundly* imbalanced

- Forgive your parents or someone you hold a grudge against.

- Create your spiritual family, and connect with them often.

- Get a full-spectrum light, and use it every day.

- Get a puppy or a kitten.

- Take a healing workshop.

- Ask for help instead of doing things alone.

- Volunteer in an AIDS ward, a soup kitchen, or an animal shelter.

- Donate your old-but-still-good suits and shoes to an "off welfare and back to work" program.

- Get Rolfed, or have deep tissue massage therapy.

- Befriend an elderly person, and offer to take him or her once a week to the grocery store or on an outing.

- Admit your weaknesses and seek support.

- *Tell* the people you love that you love them.

- Live and let live. (You never know how much time you or anyone else has.)

Remember, the heart is

Empathy
Generosity
Compassion
Forgiveness
Nurturing
Understanding
Listening
Acceptance
Tolerance
Affection
Kindness
Patience
Laughter

As you regain balance in your heart chakra, your spirit will inspire you to maintain this balance in other, more personal ways. Write your personal ideas in the space below:

_____

_____

_____

_____

Fifth Chakra

Balanced Expression

THE FIFTH CHAKRA, known as the throat chakra, is located at the back of the neck and encompasses the entire jaw. It focuses on communication, connection, creativity, and personal intention. On a physiological level, this chakra governs the throat, thyroid, trachea, esophagus, parathyroid, hypothalamus, neck, mouth, teeth, and ears; when imbalanced, it may affect the health of these areas as well. On an energy level, it is the center of personal expression; it is the channel through which we introduce our spirit to the world. On the color spectrum, this chakra vibrates energetically to the color blue like a summer sky. Its mission statement is "I express. I listen. I communicate."

When our expression is open and balanced, we are able to communicate with integrity and become a conduit for positive and uplifting energy. When our expression is fully balanced, we communicate only that which is in harmony with our spirit. We awaken to the spiritual truth that our life is built directly from our words, thoughts, beliefs, and ideas.

The fifth chakra does not only govern our ability to express ourselves creatively and effectively in life. It also governs our ability to connect with the creative expressions of others, to listen to their communication, and to lay the foundation for understanding. It is the center for negotiation, discussion, and—most important—teaching and learning. This center is our gateway to the world, moving us from our own subjective perspective to different points of view. Therefore, expression is an agent for progress and evolution. It propels us forward, inviting us to go beyond ourselves so that we may grow. It allows us to offer what we know to others, and it invites others to share what they know with us, laying the foundation for peaceful and healthy relationships, whether between individuals or groups.

On an energy level, this center acts as a chimney for the heart, conveying our real feelings to the world. When it is balanced, we are inspired to communicate uplifting and healing messages, sharing with others our highest desires. We intuitively understand the power of our words and their influences on those who hear them. We recognize that we are all interconnected, and that every expression we release into the world will have an impact, whether we want it to or not.

If, for example, you are having a bad day, you may speak to someone harshly, never actually saying anything unkind but clearly conveying your misdirected irritation. That innocent person may misinterpret your irritability as a reaction to him and become defensive and afraid. Then, because he is feeling threatened, he will speak to the next person with an edge in his voice, once again causing a negative reaction, and so on. Once set in motion, this chain effect can pollute an entire environment, adversely affecting all those who are in it, leaving everyone drained and wondering what hit them. All the while, the person with the imbalanced expression remains unconscious of what he has initiated and may even continue to wreak energetic havoc. This happens often in office environments. It takes only one person to ruin the energy for everyone.

If your expression is open and balanced, you will be mindful of how influential your communication is, and you will therefore pay attention to what you communicate. You will be sensitive to the impact your words have on those who hear them, and you will strive to communicate in such a way as to respect and honor all who hear you. Your expression is a powerful instrument of creativity when you can communicate what is in your heart without injury or disrespect. Then the very sound of your voice becomes endowed with a quality that brings harmony and balance to any situation.

YOUR MAGIC WAND

Your expression reveals to others the choices you make in life, letting them know who you are, what you care about, and the level of responsibility you are willing to take for your life. More than any other energy center, it tells the world what you intend to do with your life while you are here, while simultaneously inviting others to share their dreams with you. This center acts as a bridge builder, assisting you in establishing connections.

When your expression is balanced, you can make responsible choices that fully and honestly support all you need in order to be happy. You no longer say yes when you mean to say no, or strive to suppress your true feelings. You upgrade your level of awareness and begin to move toward what is genuine rather than acquiescing to those around you and their agendas. Your expression is the messenger of your spirit because it announces you to the world. When balanced, it allows you not only to speak your personal truth but also to live your personal truth. This is the energy center where you fully claim authority for your life, listen to your heart and intuition, and become fully present to the Divine Spirit within you. This is the center where you begin to turn inward rather than outward for direction.

People in public positions of influence and power, including teachers, politicians, ministers, and even actors, have highly developed centers of expression, which can be used for either good or ill, depending upon their intentions. Simply addressing others allows these people to greatly affect them. This can even lead to a type of devotion, which explains why some singers, actors, and other public personalities have passionate followings. Their expression commands respect and makes them very attractive. My favorite example of the power of expression is that of Mahatma Gandhi, who led India in its war of independence with only the power of his words. A true and clear channel for Divine Power, he ordered that not a single bullet be fired at the British in the name of freedom. And people complied. Speech like Gandhi's, spoken from a clear center, with clear intent and in complete alignment with the heart, is powerfully creative. It can be the equivalent of a personal magic wand.

CHECKING YOUR EXPRESSION

	Yes	No	Sometimes
I speak clearly and pronounce my words well.	———	———	———
People listen to me.	———	———	———
I react strongly to what I hear.	———	———	———
I am mindful of what I say.	———	———	———
I express my needs without losing my temper.	———	———	———
My words are powerful.	———	———	———
I listen to others without interruption.	———	———	———
I speak with optimism.	———	———	———
I am direct and forthright.	———	———	———
I am careful not to criticize unfairly.	———	———	———
I am a good negotiator.	———	———	———
People confide in me.	———	———	———
I am truthful.	———	———	———

	Yes	No	Sometimes
I compliment others freely.	_____	_____	_____
I listen to my intuition.	_____	_____	_____

If you answered no to any one of these statements, your expression is somewhat imbalanced. If you answered no to two or three statements, you are slightly imbalanced and should follow the suggestions for slight imbalances at the end of this chapter. If you answered no to four to seven statements, then your expression is moderately imbalanced, and you should follow the suggestions for adjusting moderate imbalances. If you answered no to eight or more statements, then your expression is seriously shut down. You should follow the suggestions for serious imbalances in order to help you retrieve your expression and become more powerful and creative.

TUNING IN TO YOUR PSYCHIC RADIO

Expression acts as a three-way psychic radio. The first band activates your speaking and listening abilities. When the first band is connecting effectively and you are listening to someone, you might nod in agreement or say something like "I understand" or "Yeah, I know what you mean" to indicate that you are in rapport. Their words just seem to flow, and you actually hear whatever is said. When this band is open and balanced, you are able to understand not only the communication of those around you but, more important, the intention behind that communication, activating your ability to empathize.

This band of expression also governs all forms of creativity, awakening your ability to connect with others, using whatever means feels natural. Some will rely on words to share what is in their hearts. Others will turn to art, dancing, playing music, acting, singing, or even touching; simply holding hands can be a very powerful way to communicate.

The second band establishes mental and telepathic rapport with others. It both sends and receives thoughts and feelings, especially from those who are on the same wavelength as you are. You know the second band of the throat chakra is activated when someone next to you begins to sing the song that has been silently running through your mind for hours. Or when someone you've been thinking about, such as your mother who lives two states away, phones you at the very moment you were thinking about her. This band is operating when you are looking for something, and someone else just offers it to you out of the blue.

I had a client who was working on a difficult research project on musical instruments in the Middle Ages. He went to the library to look for a particular book on the subject, and although the book was listed on the computer, it wasn't where it was supposed to be on the shelf, and no one could find it. He was told that a search would be made and he should return the next day. The next day he was informed that the book could not be found. Completely frustrated, he asked, "What could possibly have happened to it?" Before the librarian could even venture a guess, a little old lady walked up to the desk, handed the librarian a large book, and said, "I found this in the anatomy section, and I don't think it belongs there." It was the very book they had been searching for! Absolutely amazed, the librarian handed it to my client.

Coincidences such as these occur under the domain of the second band of the throat chakra, which acts as a subtle psychic relay station working to achieve harmony and rapport at all times. This aspect of expression is the engine behind the synchronicities that occur in life. The positive side of this is that often our way is made easier when we tune in to others. The downside is the possibility that we may tune in to thoughts that do not reflect our real feelings or truly benefit us. When this happens, we actually lose power because we parrot the thoughts of others and not those of our spirit.

For example, you may tune in to the common belief at your workplace that a vacation of two weeks is frowned upon. You may not have had any personal communication from a superior that such vacations are frowned upon, but because you tune in to this idea, you may limit your vacation to one week for fear that you might lose your job. This belief may have been floating around for a long time. Maybe it reflects an older management's point of view. Maybe it was expressed at one time to someone in particular. Maybe it is just a myth floating in the collective thought pool. But if you tune in to it, you will begin to think the collective thoughts and when it comes to planning your vacation, you may cheat yourself out of deeper relaxation or a more exotic destination.

Collective thoughts can have more serious and damaging effects. They are responsible for perpetuating the racial biases and intolerant beliefs that keep us suspicious and afraid of one another. I call collective thought "junk thought." The best way not to fall under its influence is to be aware of your feelings, thoughts, and beliefs. If your feelings can be supported by your experience or if you can explain why you feel the way you do, then you are not hooked into collective thought. If, however, your ability to back up your feelings is vague, rethink them. Perhaps you are just carrying around a lot of junk thought. The clearer you are about what you think, the higher the level of mental and telepathic rapport you will establish with others. If you lack direction, you risk getting pulled into the undertow of mass thinking. If you feel this happens to you, pay attention to your thoughts. Ask yourself, "Do I really feel this way, or is it just a collective junk thought that I'm reflecting? Do I have any personal experience to back up my feeling?" And finally, check with yourself before you speak. Many times we say things that we do not genuinely feel but instead speak out of laziness, habit, or to fill a silence.

Do you "get" what people say? Do you easily understand what they mean?

_____

Are you able to establish instant rapport? With whom? When was the last time?

_____

_____

Do you misunderstand others or feel misunderstood by others frequently? About what?

_____

_____

What is your most powerful form of communication? Art? Writing? Speaking? Playing music? Touch?

_____

_____

THE HIGHER OCTAVE

The third and highest band of psychic expression tunes in to our own inner voice; it picks up our intuition and our spirit guides and angels. If your expression is awakened and fully functioning, you are able to tell the difference between your own muddled mind-chatter, the endless drone of confusion that arises from our egos as we struggle to feel safe and in control in our lives, and the lucid and loving communication of your soul, gently guiding you to pay attention to the deeper meaning of life. This band of expression awakens your connection to your own spirit and begins to direct you toward the very highest kinds of expression.

This band opens up the psychic gift of clairaudience, or "clear hearing." Clairaudience is the ability to tune in to the Divine Spirit for direction at any given moment. When this aspect of expression is activated, we are guided to make the best possible decisions. Clairaudience also channels our spirit guides, who are ready to assist us in every possible way. When this channel of expression is open, we are in constant contact with Higher Power; we can navigate through life so that we may experience all its beauty while avoiding the pitfalls. When we are in tune with Spirit, we are in a state of grace. We seem to draw to us just what we need rather than having to go after it. This band of expression brings an almost magical quality to life, offering gifts in the form of subtle impulses, hunches, instincts, and bright ideas. The fifth chakra reminds us that we are Divine children of heaven, who are watched over and cared for every step of the way.

The most direct way to activate the third band of expression, where our intuition resides, is to consciously bring our choices into alignment with our hearts. This means we stop asking other people what they think about our decisions and get into the habit of asking our Higher Self instead. Taking time out during the day for meditation or contemplation also quiets the mental chatter that constantly rumbles through the brain and frees us to hear the voice of our intuition. Initially this may require some effort, but eventually it becomes more natural as we come to recognize and appreciate our intuition's quiet response, its calming vibration, and its quiet inner tone. The key to intuition is to know that this broadcast from our soul is always present and available. We do not "turn it on." Eliminating distractions frees us up to hear its subtle guidance.

Do you get gut feelings, hunches, or other messages from your spirit?

_____

Do you often shop your ideas around for input from others? Whom do you ask for input most often? Is their input beneficial?

_____

_____

Are you plagued with endless mind-chatter? Voices of doubt? Voices of "what if"? How big a problem is this?

_____

Have you ever experienced telepathy?

_____

_____

Have you tuned in to "junk thought"? Are you buying into ideas and beliefs float-ing around the atmosphere of your workplace or home? How do these junk thoughts make you feel?

_____

_____

ACCESSING YOUR INTUITION

Our intuition is not, of course, an audible voice, although for many it becomes just as distinct. Because it is a subtle broadcast, we need to put ourselves in the right frame of mind to perceive it. The best way to do this is to make four basic decisions that will convey to your subconscious mind that you intend to honor your intuition and pay attention to it as it arises. The first of these decisions is that you will be *open* to being an intuitive person. This decision sets up your mind to be receptive to your intuition rather than ignoring it. Ask yourself: Am I open to intuitive feelings? Do I think of myself as an intuitive person? Am I mentally will-ing to be flexible and allow for intuition to influence my behavior? An attitude of openness sets the stage for intuitive awakening. It takes you beyond mere interest in intuition and creates the possibility for your own intuition to activate.

The second decision is even more intentional than the first. Once you become open to being intuitive, you must come to actually *expect* it. This may feel presumptuous, but if you recognize intuition as the natural expression of a balanced fifth chakra and the voice of your Higher Self, expecting to be intuitive makes sense. Expectation acts as a magnet for intuitive feelings. Those who expect to be intuitive will be, and those who don't expect to be usually won't be. Or at least they won't recognize and value their intuitive feelings as important. Ask yourself: "How often do I check in with my intuition when I must make decisions? When I do get an intuitive 'hit,' how do I react? Do I accept it as natural? Or do I react as if it is unnatural?" Expecting to be intuitive serves as a powerful catalyst for heightened awareness.

The third decision is to *trust* your intuitive feelings when they do arise. This may be more challenging, because your intuitive feelings may not be supported by appearances or confirmed by others. They may even be in conflict with your beliefs at times. Coming to trust your intuition isn't as difficult as you may think, however, especially if you use the following suggestion. Get a small pocket notebook, and every time you have a gut feeling, a hunch, an "aha" feeling, or any intuitive impulse, simply jot it down. Don't censor, judge, reason, or evaluate these feelings one way or another. Just notice and record them. Once you begin your intuition notebook, check it every couple of days. As you look over your entries, ask yourself: "Did my intuition on this or that matter have merit? Did my intuition help me? Did I trust it? Should I have trusted it?" It is far easier to trust your intuition if you have evidence that it is trustworthy. Your pocket notebook will most definitely prove that it is.

The fourth and most important decision in balancing your fifth chakra is to *act* on your intuition when it guides you, especially if it doesn't intrude upon or harm anyone in any way. Every time you act on your intuition, you are suggesting to your subconscious mind that you value your intuitive feelings and want them to flow easily into your conscious realm of attention. Ask yourself: "Do I follow my hunches when they arise? Do I listen to my gut instincts when faced with decisions? Do I allow my intuition to guide me?"

Making these four basic decisions—to be open, to expect, to trust, and to act on intuitive feelings—will create a direct conduit for your fifth chakra to communicate messages to you, both from your Higher Self and from your angels and guides, at all times.

What was your most recent intuitive feeling?

_____

_____

_____

In what area of your life are you most intuitive? At work? With family? In health matters? Other?

_____

_____

_____

Can you recall a specific time when your intuition helped you? How?

_____

_____

Do you check with your intuition on important matters?

_____

_____

Can you recall a time when you acted on your intuition?

_____

_____

BE SILENT

Some time ago I discovered that a beautiful way to activate intuition and strengthen the throat chakra is to practice silence. By remaining silent for a period of time during the day, I found that I raised my level of awareness of both what I said to myself and what others said to me. When I took a break from mindless chatter, suddenly the world filled up with a richness of song and sound that had completely escaped me before. Now, whenever I'm feeling overloaded, I stroll through my own neighborhood, actively listening to the birds singing, the cars passing, the airplanes flying overhead, the children playing in the street. As I begin to connect to this wonderfully rich world going on around me, my mood immediately lifts. I step out of my mental chatter, back into the big, bright, beautiful, and endlessly exciting world that I live in. Doing this never fails to put my life in perspective and inspires me in creative new ways to look at old things. Mostly it reminds me of the power of inner dialogue. We can get so entranced with what we tell ourselves about life that we literally cut ourselves off from actually experiencing life. Practicing silence frees us up and gives us a way to rejoin the rest of the world. I can see why monks like silence so much. It's absolutely liberating!

Another balancing practice is to engage in some sort of artistic expression on a daily basis, whether it is creative writing, playing the piano, painting a watercolor, or baking a pie. When you relax into creative expression, the mind rests and the heart opens, moving its loving energy through the fifth chakra and out into the world. Taking up a new creative art form allows you the thrill of expressing yourself in a new way.

You can also activate your intuition if you give up worrying about how other people perceive you. The truth is, everyone is so preoccupied with their own lives that they rarely pay much attention to anyone else for more than a glancing moment or two. Unless you are a main player in someone else's life, the rule is generally "out of sight, out of mind." So don't waste precious energy worrying about how other people perceive you. Listening to and following your own inner voice will ease your insecurities. It will also provide you with a more accurate picture of others. This will reveal that other people are basically like you, wanting the same things: love, comfort, and acceptance. Knowing this, the world will become a friendlier place.

TRY THIS!

Breathe When Talking

Whenever you are speaking with someone, focus on your breath. Make sure you aren't holding it. As you listen, breathe in and out, and allow your shoulders to relax. This will release any defensiveness you are holding. Doing this will also open up your expression and allow you to receive more of the content and intent of the person speaking to you. Conversely, whenever you are exposed to negative talk, hold your breath and turn your face away so that you are not exposed to negative thoughts and ideas. This remedy can be tricky to do without being obvious, but it's possible if you practice. While looking the other way, send the offending person "good vibes" and kind thoughts if you can. Doing this will protect you even more.

TRY THIS!

Speaking from the Heart

The next time you have a discussion with someone who is difficult to talk to or with whom you have a difficult time agreeing, gently place your hand over your heart as you speak and as you listen. As you do so, hold the intention to speak and listen with an open heart and a nonjudgmental desire to connect and understand in a positive way. This technique is a cue to both your subconscious mind and your body to remain balanced, calm, receptive, and interested in hearing what the other person is saying to you. It will strengthen and improve your communication and indicate to the person you are speaking with that you are willing to value their point of view. This is usually all it takes to overcome impasses in communication.

NOURISHMENT

The fifth chakra is located where food, drink, drugs, smoke, and other external substances enter our bodies. Our choices here determine whether we ingest healthy and wholesome substances or whether instead we poison ourselves. If we align our willpower (the third center) with our desire to express our best possible selves, the choices we make to feed and sustain ourselves will be sane, smart, and nourishing. But if our expression is weak and we make self-destructive choices in how we sustain ourselves, we create problems both for ourselves and for others, who in the end often have to rescue us.

On the mental level, what we feed our mind and soul is just as important as what we feed our body. Our spirit needs to be given loving, inspiring, and nurturing thoughts that uplift us and help us feel supported in the world. People who live on a steady diet of violent movies, exploitative television shows, tabloid newspapers, and depressing talk radio programs will diminish the power of the fifth chakra just as surely as do those who overindulge in sweets and alcohol.

My mother told me a wonderful story that shows how teaching a person to use expression correctly can heal them, both physically and emotionally, in a remarkably short period of time. Because my mother came to America after the war and understands very well the challenges of adjusting to a new country, both she and my father, as part of their spiritual path, have committed to helping older immigrants who have recently arrived in the Denver area. They often take them to the grocery store or to the doctor, or sometimes just on an outing to the mountains of Colorado. Last spring my mother received a call about a seventy-nine-year-old Hungarian woman named Suzan who had no family or relatives and was sinking fast. She had terrible arthritis, was having trouble concentrating, and was extremely depressed. She didn't drive, lived on canned soup, couldn't get out much, and had very little money to live on. For my mom, these were marching orders from God. She and my father immediately went to visit Suzan and see what they could do. When they arrived, they found a frail old lady with very little spirit left. She was defensive, negative, and obviously very afraid.

Happy to meet my parents, she instantly began to tell them how hard her life was, but before she could get very far, my mother interrupted her. She said, "Suzan, I'd like to help you get well, but my suggestions for health and well-being are a little bit peculiar. I'm going to put you on a 'feast and fast' diet. For the feasting, I want you to eat a strictly vegetarian diet with lots of fresh, whole foods. And for the fasting part, my spirit [which is how my mother refers to her Higher Power, with which she is in constant contact] insists that you absolutely give up talking about your difficult and painful past. I'm sure all you have to say is true, but it is only true as of yesterday. Today is a new day, and there is no point in creating more unpleasantness by continuing to talk about the past. We'll have to find something more interesting to talk about than how miserable you feel. If you'll agree with this recipe for health, we can help you. It's up to you."

Suzan was taken aback but desperately wanted the support. "Okay," she said, laughing, "it is peculiar, but why not?" My parents began visiting her twice a week, taking her to the store, out to the movies, to the doctor, to lunch, or to a spiritual class my mother was teaching. During their visits, every time Suzan began complaining, my mother would hold up her hand like a traffic cop and say, "Suzan, my spirit doesn't want to hear this. It's a beautiful day; we're here in the moment. Your negative tales do you and me no good. They are powerful creations, and they only create more misery. Please stop."

Whenever my mom did this, Suzan would smirk. After all, she had nearly eighty years of training in speaking about everything that was wrong under the sun. Reversing herself took an incredible act of willpower and a great deal of reminding from my mom. But day by day, Suzan slowly began to change her thinking habits, her speaking habits, and her eating habits. And subtly, she began to heal. Her energy picked up. Her depression lifted. Her arthritis all but disappeared. Six months later, on her eightieth birthday, my parents threw her a party, and during the course of the evening, she danced with everyone who attended. "I feel younger now than when I was fifty," said Suzan. "Your recipe for health has really worked wonders."

The last time Suzan went to the doctor, he came out of the examination room and gave my mom a big hug. "I don't know what you're doing with her," he said, "but I'm absolutely amazed. You've taken her from death's door and shaved thirty years off her. Do you want to work for me? I need a miracle worker around here." My mom laughed and said, "It's true that a miracle has happened. The miracle is that Suzan's thinking has changed. She no longer creates with her words what she doesn't want. She claims the life she does want. God gives us life in the package that we ask for. She simply asked for better."

The power that arises from our throat chakra is awesome, whether we realize it or not. When we align our actual words and, more important, our mental dialogue with our highest good, nothing can stop us from creating a balanced and healthy life. As my mother reminds me over and over again, "Jesus said, 'Don't you know that you are God's?' As you speak it, think it, swallow it, so it is."

What do you feed your body? How healthy is your diet?

_____

_____

What do you feed your mind? What kind of movies do you watch? What books do you read?

_____

_____

What do you feed the world? What things do you say about others? About yourself? About life in general?

_____

_____

_____

 TRY THIS!

Express the Good

For an entire day, choose to be the bearer of good news. Every time you speak to someone, let it be of something pleasant, something kind, or something joyful. When asked, for example, "How are you?" instead of reciting the usual mindless litany of complaints, offer a positive, upbeat response, and while you are at it, compliment the person you are speaking to. No matter how miserable you may feel at that moment, resist the temptation to "sing the blues," and make a conscious effort to notice and acknowledge what is good about the day.

IMBALANCED EXPRESSION

When your expression is imbalanced, you often suppress your true feelings. You may build walls around yourself to block input from others and live with great levels of secrecy, frustration, anger, and anxiety. You may also hide behind a false countenance and go to great lengths to conceal the hurt, pain, and anger you feel inside. Usually people who have imbalanced expression were muffled a great deal in childhood. They were often told by their parents and caretakers, either directly or indirectly, to "shut up" or "be quiet." This would be especially true when discussing the unhealthy behavior of family members.

Dysfunctional family behavior is usually shrouded in secrecy or denied. When confronted with these messages, children retreat in shame, fear, and confusion. Those who come from families where one or both parents had alcoholic or other addictive behaviors are often left with no choice but to shut down as a means of survival. When this happens, the joyful and creative spirit in the child is wounded, and the psyche withdraws. This very sad condition is one of the reasons for so much violence and misery in the world. The angry inner child eventually begins to speak, and when it does, it usually wants revenge—directed outward against others, or directed inward against the self in destructive or addictive behaviors. If your expression is thwarted, you may feel as though you are not fully present, that you are a mere facade, a paper doll, rather than a whole person of flesh and blood. Something in your voice will not ring true when you speak. You may avoid eye contact when communicating as an added protective measure. In severe cases, you may also develop speech and hearing difficulties.

I had a client, Brad, who was born to two very alcoholic, rage-aholic parents who were unable to care for him in any responsible way. The first seven years of Brad's life were hellish, characterized by almost nightly battles between his parents, along with frequent and sudden moves that completely disrupted his schooling. Brad was finally put in a foster home until he was twelve, then went to live with his grandmother until he left for college.

Because Brad's early life was so rage filled and oppressed, he learned to adapt by literally keeping his mouth shut. He rarely said anything to anyone, and when he did, it was almost inaudible. To make matters of communication worse for him, he developed an almost crippling stutter. When I met him, he could hardly utter a sentence. But in an attempt to balance his profound difficulties in communicating, he had developed a rich inner world, becoming a prolific writer of poetry, much of which focused on his dark and angry feelings. This outlet was so successful for him that he was frequently published and was even gaining some celebrity.

When I met Brad, it was as though there were no one home. His energy was weak. He offered almost nothing of himself that I could connect to. The first and second bands of his throat chakra were shattered from childhood trauma, but the third band, the one that connected him to his intuition and spirit, was operating just fine. That's why he could write so freely. I suggested to Brad that he take an experiential workshop where, with the help of a counselor, he could learn to express his feelings and heal his anger. I also suggested one-on-one speech coaching to help him develop the ability to speak his truth. Because he was so determined to free himself from his misery, he took my suggestions and made tremendous progress in opening up his throat chakra. Once he gained some confidence, he even tried reading his poetry at a poetry slam. Although he hated the experience, he loved the fact that he was able to do it.

Were you able to speak freely in your home as a child?

_____

Were the adults in your childhood open and honest in their expression?

_____

_____

Do you have difficulty speaking freely today?

_____

_____

TRY THIS!

Nighttime Messenger

Just before going to bed, write down any unexpressed feelings or communications that you were unable to successfully convey during the day. Before you sleep, ask your angels and guides to deliver these messages to those with whom you wish to connect in their dream state, as they sleep, and to return to you in your dream state any messages they may have for you. Then release your feelings and go to sleep peacefully.

RECKLESS EXPRESSION

If some people suffer from thwarted expression, others suffer from expressing themselves recklessly. Such people talk on and on mindlessly, communicating little of any real substance. They use talking as a means of distancing themselves and avoiding intimate connection with others. Inane and aimless talk may also be a way of tuning out negative mind-chatter. When your expression is reckless, you may grate on people's nerves, consume their energy, and bore them.

I had a client, Louise, whose expression was completely reckless. From the minute she walked into my office to the minute she left, she talked nonstop, leaving me absolutely no opportunity to get a word in edgewise. She indulged in idle gossip, criticism, and extravagant indictments of everyone she knew. Underneath it all, Louise was an unhappy, self-absorbed, and lonely woman who didn't possess the skills of listening to or connecting with others. She was a child of a very dysfunctional family where everyone seemed to be the expert, no one made mistakes, and if there was ever a problem, it was always someone else's fault. In that environment, no one ever listened to her. Rather than shut down, as Brad did, Louise modeled the behavior of those around her and became a loudmouthed know-it-all kid who grew into a very loudmouthed know-it-all adult. She couldn't be told a thing. She corrected everyone she came in contact with, from the mailman who couldn't deliver the mail correctly, to the dry cleaner who could never press her clothing well enough, to the grocery clerk who didn't bag groceries properly, and on and on. Her expression blocked everyone else's, and she was left isolated in her own world because it allowed for no one else. To balance her expression, Louise needed to stop talking and listen—something she found very difficult to do because her experience as a child told her listening wasn't valued. Even more important, learning wasn't valued, because we learn when we listen.

Another client, Amy, had the same problem as Louise, although it was far less obvious. Amy is the type of woman who does everything perfectly. She is a highly successful businesswoman who negotiates million-dollar deals with clients around the world, and she also gives dinner parties that would be the envy of Martha Stewart. She is the first to send a birthday card or give a compliment or a little present. And yet, as lovely and gracious as she is, communicating with her was always very frustrating. Like Louise, she did all the talking. And like Louise, it didn't take much for her to start complaining about everyone she knew. Her conversations centered exclusively on her life, her interests, and her problems.

She never asked any questions about the person she was speaking to, and if she did, she was quick to interrupt because she wasn't really listening. After my first few sessions with her, I felt somehow exhausted and slightly irritated. I soon identified the problem as an overbearing expression. No wonder I felt frustrated. Speaking with her didn't build bridges. It built only a platform for her performance. Others were merely members of her audience. She confided several times that she was tired and angry and felt she was doing all the work of creating a meaningful life, not only for herself but also for her friends and her husband. In her case, however, the problem was not that others didn't want to express and share their experiences with her. It was that she didn't allow them to.

Both Amy and Louise had to learn to modify their expression by practicing self-control. They had to concentrate on actually connecting with others when they spoke. I suggested that they focus on their breathing and consciously take in information and energy while listening to others. This focus helped them to resist their inclination to interrupt people—a hard habit to break, especially for Louise. I also suggested that she see Patrick, my husband, for meditation instruction, and that she receive massage therapy, during which time she could not speak. She now has weekly meditation sessions with Patrick as well as twice-monthly bodywork with a therapist, and she slowly is beginning to see a change. I also suggested to both women that they consider attending a twelve-step support group, such as Al-Anon or ACOA, which helps people create healthy relationship dynamics, or CODA, a twelve-step group for people who overdo for others and neglect to care for themselves. In such groups, you are required to listen to others speak without interruption and share your own experiences without lengthy self-disclosure. The best part is that no discussion about what is said in the group is permitted. The process of listening without commentary and keeping your own comments brief is very healing for those with an imbalanced expression chakra. If this is your problem, chances are you may not even be aware of it. But if you've been told you talk too much, or if you are accused of never listening, perhaps your expression needs to be toned down a bit. The same remedies would be helpful for you.

Are you inclined to talk or to listen when communicating with others?

_____

Are you guilty of gossiping about others?

_____

Are you open to learning from others?

_____

Do you talk just to fill the silence?

_____

TRY THIS!

Put the Spotlight on Others

For one day, consciously take the focus off yourself and place it on the people around you instead. Give others your full attention when they speak to you, and show interest and enthusiasm in what they are saying. Refrain from talking much about yourself during this day, but instead ask others meaningful questions and cheer them on in their undertakings. (Make certain as you do this, however, that you do not confuse showing interest and listening with the need to solve problems or rescue others, for this will only get you into trouble.)

EXPLOSION/IMPLOSION

Another common imbalance of expression is the habit of refraining from expressing our needs or establishing our boundaries for fear that it might offend others. Surprisingly, this particular condition afflicts even the most powerful and successful of people.

I had a client, David, who was one of the most well-respected international advertising executives in the world. In fact, in many circles he was the symbol of good business communication. Yet in his personal life, in a third marriage, he was walked over by his wife's family. He could not seem to communicate his real needs or establish boundaries to save his soul. He and his wife, Meg, had barely moved into their carefully designed new home, a lifelong dream for David, when her freeloading thirty-five-year-old son, Harold, showed up and moved in without permission from either David or Meg. Although David never discussed what was going on, he intuitively felt that his wife was concerned about Harold, that she wished he would grow up, and that she probably didn't want Harold there any more than he did. Yet David was resentful because she didn't stop Harold from intruding on them and never even talked about the situation. Frustrated and annoyed, David nevertheless said nothing for fear that he would appear selfish or insensitive. He wanted desperately to avoid causing problems with his wife. So he bit his tongue and hoped Harold would leave on his own. Unfortunately, that didn't happen. Harold ignored all of David's hints and even invited friends in on weekends, including a girlfriend who also showed no signs of ever leaving. The last straw, however, was the arrival of a pair of Doberman pinschers, who of course had the run of the house. David finally became infuriated and threw Harold out—dogs, girlfriend, and all. Frightened by her husband's display of rage, Meg left with them. Because their marriage was so weakened by the lack of any real communication, it broke apart. Meg never came back. To add to David's misery, ten weeks after their separation, he was diagnosed with polyps in his throat and had to have immediate surgery to remove them.

I helped David see that both his physical condition and his emotional problems were connected to his repressed expression. His failed third marriage was just another example of how costly this problem can be. Once he realized how devastated he was, both psychically and physically, he knew he had to make a change. His losses taught him that it was finally time to learn to communicate more openly instead of leaving it up to others to guess what his needs were. On the suggestion of his private therapist, David began group therapy. From the feedback I've received, it's helping enormously. He is learning to be more direct in his personal communication, just as he is in his business affairs. His throat—and his throat chakra are now on the mend.

Learning to speak your mind is especially difficult when it comes to expressing anger. Many of us are taught that being angry—and even worse, expressing it—is impolite and unacceptable. Unfortunately, people who have a hard time expressing anger often attract people who are all too good at expressing it. This seems to be the Universe's way of organizing us so that we can teach each other about balance. In these situations, we may feel that we can't say anything to those who anger us, for fear the repercussions would be too great. For example, if we work for an oppressive boss or have an abusive spouse or parent, we may feel as though we don't have a voice. And so we keep our fifth chakra bottled up. The truth is, there is nothing inappropriate about having feelings and expressing them. What is unrealistic is expecting others to understand our needs telepathically. It is our psychic responsibility to understand what we need and to communicate this before we blow up and scare everyone half to death, as David did.

Even worse, repressing the fifth chakra can cause people to implode. I had a client whose daughter, Emily, was a soft-spoken, gentle girl. She was a conservative Catholic with a strong interest in humanitarian pursuits; she dreamed of doing missionary or social work as a vocation. When she went away to college, she was assigned a roommate who was very different from any girl she had known before. A child of aging hippies, her roommate was a promiscuous, dope-smoking, wild child who seemed to be majoring in sex. Every night she invited in a new boy, often coming in at well past midnight and carrying on with her partner till dawn, all in a ten-by-twelve-foot room. The situation was unbearable for Emily. She couldn't study. She couldn't sleep. Her personal space was completely invaded, and her values were being trampled upon. Nevertheless, since she was afraid to express her anger, she bit her tongue and only gave her roommate dirty looks, never confronting her directly about her behavior. Day in and day out the tension increased, and Emily became more and more frustrated. In November, Emily suddenly awoke one night to her roommate's antics and found she had a terrible sore throat. She couldn't speak. She couldn't swallow. She could hardly breathe for the pain. Desperate, she dressed and went to the school clinic, where she was referred to a throat specialist, who immediately diagnosed a severe case of tonsillitis.

When Emily came home, she cried, "Mom, I have such a bad sore throat, I can hardly speak. My throat is screaming in pain." The minute she heard Emily say this, my client, a spiritually conscious mother, said, "Emily, I am not surprised this is happening. Do you realize that's exactly what you've been saying to me for the past two months? Every time we've talked about your roommate, you've said the same thing: 'I want to scream. I can hardly speak, I'm so angry.' Now it's taken over your body. Your throat is expressing your anger for you."

Emily had a tonsillectomy over Christmas break, and after talking to her mother about her situation, she made an emergency request to the dean to change roommates. When she explained why, the dean agreed to a change. Happily settled in a new dorm room and making new friends, Emily vowed never again to repress her feelings to such an extent. "I've learned my lesson," she said to her mom. "I'm committed to speaking up from now on. After two months of psychic torture, I'm determined to say what's on my mind no matter what!"

How effective are you in communicating your frustrations?

_____

_____

Do you blow up? Over what?

_____

_____

Do others blow up at you?

_____

_____

Are you in the habit of bottling up your feelings? Do you hold back what you
need to say? With everyone? Or just some people? Who?

_____

_____

TRY THIS!

Speak Up!

The moment you feel that someone is disrespecting your boundaries,
offending you, or not hearing you, speak up and tell him or her how it
affects you *physically*. Do not accuse him or her of insensitive or unacceptable behavior or attempt to change them in any way. Simply reveal
how their actions affect you, in as neutral a way as possible. For example, when someone offends you, after checking with your body, you
might say, "Gee, when you say [whatever was said], or do [whatever was
done], my throat tightens, and my body feels as though it wants to run in
the opposite direction as fast as it can." The key to this remedy is to
reveal only your physical experience and nothing more. Even though this
is a very peculiar way of communicating, it almost always succeeds in
getting the other person to recognize and acknowledge his or her impact
on you. (Of course, this remedy may not be appropriate at work, or in
more volatile relationships, but with most personal relationships, such as
with lovers, spouses, family, and children, it works very well.)

 TRY THIS!

Peppermint Splash

A lovely remedy for opening up expression and refreshing this energy center is to drink a glass of peppermint water. Add one drop of peppermint essential oil to a glass of spring water. The peppermint cleanses the throat of mucus and clears away all psychic debris. It is especially helpful when you are about to deliver an important speech or have a meaningful conversation with someone. I suggest you use only the finest grade of essential oil for this remedy because cheaper brands are often diluted with other oils, making them harmful to the throat. Find a store that sells essential oils, and ask the advice of the salespeople there. They are usually very well informed and can direct you to the best product.

SPEAK WITHOUT INFLICTING INJURY

One of the greatest misuses of expression is invalidating another person through blame, shame, or injurious name-calling. Often people resort to yelling when they feel they are not being heard. In response, they are either totally dismissed or their message is drowned out in the barrage of angry words hurled back in retaliation. Throwing around such negative messages causes significant psychic damage to both sides.

I had a client, Bill, who was very frustrated because his wife, Lisa, never listened to him. She constantly interrupted and didn't seem to care about anything he said. Lisa, on the other hand, said that Bill spoke in an abrupt, judgmental, and blaming fashion and so she had to resort to shouting to get heard. The two were locked in a battle that got louder and louder over the years as they had fight after frustrating fight. After each episode, they both felt as though they had been beaten up. Lisa's energy level dropped so low, she thought she had chronic fatigue syndrome, and Bill was so drained that he had no desire to do anything when he got home but watch TV to numb his injured feelings. Desperate to save their marriage, they finally went for help.

Through counseling, they learned that in order to be heard, they needed to speak in nonthreatening ways and use nonaccusatory language. They also had to want to hear what each other said; they needed to listen actively, something they both agreed would be new for them. Paying better attention to their ways of communicating gradually allowed their relationship to improve. Today they are speaking to each other instead of simply yelling.

Do you have the habit of arguing or fighting with people in your life?

_____

_____

When you grew up, did your parents fight or argue with each other? Were they verbally abusive?

_____

_____

Are you verbally abusive? To others? To yourself?

_____

_____

Do you have the habit of interrupting when someone is speaking?

_____

_____

 TRY THIS!

Criticism Fast

Here's a remedy that my friend, author Alan Cohen, suggests. Avoid criticizing anyone or complaining about anything for one day. This especially includes criticizing yourself. You will need to pay great attention to how you speak and think, which may be easier if you spend the day with a supportive friend who can point to any digressions. Enjoy the freedom from negative creations that comes with this restraint. If you are successful for a day, try extending it to two days, three days, even a week. Let your own experience be your incentive to keep it up.

A corollary to this practice is to not correct anyone else in any way, either verbally or mentally. In other words, give up being the boss of the Universe, telling everyone how to "do life" according to you. Your own throat chakra is freed when you stop trying to choke anyone else's.

WISHY-WASHY

Another version of an imbalanced expression is to play both sides of every situation. This could mean, for example, being a friend to someone when you are with him or her, only to abandon all loyalty the minute you leave. It's being a "fair-weather friend," "two faced," or a "wimp." It's what Native Americans called speaking with a "forked tongue." Whatever it is called, it means not having your own truth. You end up feeling like a psychic parasite, because you literally feed off the energy of others.

If this seems familiar, you need to become aware that your expression has evaporated and that you are suffering greatly for it. To heal this condition, you may have to engage the help of a qualified therapist to help you find your truth and awaken your personal voice. You can also journal or join a therapy group where you can feel safe expressing your own ideas. The problem may be just one of laziness in connecting to what you care about and finding the courage to express it. In any case, find the courage to express what you really feel, and if you are in doubt, say nothing at all. Once you do state something, do not abandon it or betray yourself just to gain temporary approval from others. It's not getting someone else's approval that will make you feel better. It's your own.

Are you wishy-washy? Do you easily reverse your position on matters just to keep the peace?

_____

_____

What are you afraid of in speaking your own mind?

_____

_____

Have you ever taken a stand and remained firm in your position? On what?

_____

_____

Do you agree with others outwardly when you really feel otherwise? Or vice versa? When?

_____

_____

SAY WHAT YOU MEAN

One of the greatest misuses of expression is to slander someone or to manipulate others into doing the same. In fact, this is such a serious transgression that it is laid out as one of the Ten Commandments: "Thou shall not bear false witness." Not only does slander compromise your vibration and integrity, but your words also have a boomerang effect—they will come back to haunt you. If you think you can say something that maligns another's character and get away with it, you are only kidding yourself.

This point was driven home in my family just recently. For our two preteen daughters, the focus of the world is who is popular and who isn't. Though it is important that we come to find our place in the world, the popularity game can be very damaging, as one of my daughters discovered. Sabrina was caught up in a threesome at school, in which she and two other girls in her class maneuvered endlessly to be one-up. Almost every day, not surprisingly, one of them was in the unhappy position of being the odd girl out. This jockeying for position hit a whole new level of misery when Cissy phoned Sabrina and began discussing the other girl, Jolene, with her. At first the conversation seemed benign enough, but eventually Cissy egged Sabrina on to say something unkind about Jolene. Unknown to Sabrina, Cissy had Jolene on the other line, and she heard every word Sabrina said. "Hey, that's mean," Jolene interjected. Then Cissy laughed and said, "See, Jolene, I told you Sabrina wasn't your friend," and hung up the phone. Feeling ambushed, embarrassed by her own unkind words, and overwhelmed at the manipulation involved, Sabrina came crying to me.

Though we were certainly frustrated with Cissy's trap, it was important for Sabrina to realize that her own words were the source of her misery. Although the sting was painful and her embarrassment was huge, Sabrina learned her lesson. Saying something hateful or unkind does get back to you—if not directly, as in Sabrina's case, then energetically. We must not underestimate the power of our words. Throwing mean-spirited words into the world about anyone is a spiritual assault. In keeping with the rule "what goes around comes around," your words will come back to you. Count on it.

Respect the age-old adage "If you cannot say anything nice, better to say nothing at all." To that, I'd like to add, "If you wouldn't say it directly to a person, don't say it at all." Though this is nearly impossible to follow, as we all love to gossip, it is worth striving for. Another, more livable directive is to follow the Zen precept "Say what you can live with."

Have you ever been hung by your own words? In what way?

_____

_____

Have you ever embarrassed yourself by getting caught in a lie or slander?

_____

_____

Have you ever said something unkind or untrue about someone and didn't get caught? How did you feel about yourself afterward?

_____

_____

WORDS CREATE

One of the most important things to understand about expression is its power to create your life. Our subconscious mind is programmed to accept absolutely all that we suggest to it, and the two most powerful words we can utter to the subconscious mind are the words *"I am."* When we say "I am," we are commanding the Universe to manifest all that we utter. Therefore, if we say, "I am tired," our bodies, which respond to our subconscious mind, will say, "Okay. You said tired. Here's tired." The same holds true for "I am sick"; "I am poor"; "I am lonely"; "I am unhealthy"; "I am happy"; "I am invigorated"; "I am loved and lovable." In other words, your expression claims the truth of who you are. Whatever you command will come to pass, good or bad, when using the magic words *"I am,"* if you invoke them consistently enough.

Knowing this, you can direct your words to create your life to fulfill your desires. Fifteen years ago, my husband, Patrick, decided he didn't want to continue to damage his health by smoking and that he wanted to quit. A smoker since the age of fourteen, he was quite challenged by this desire. So he decided to use the power of his words. Whenever he wanted a cigarette, he took in a deep breath and said to himself, "I prefer health." Whenever anyone offered him a cigarette—which was often in those days, as we were surrounded by lots of smokers—he simply said, "No thank you, I am a nonsmoker." And from the day he decided to quit, he was a nonsmoker. When I asked him if quitting was difficult, he said, "No. Why should I create it being difficult by telling myself it is? As a nonsmoker, it takes no effort at all." I was so impressed at how he managed to break a twenty-year habit that I too decided to quit. Using the same method, I kicked the habit in a day. We've both been smoke-free ever since.

The best way to take advantage of your creative and healing power is to practice invoking exactly what you desire through the use of affirmation. The subconscious mind, which executes your creative orders, responds best to repeated statements. Create simple statements that affirm exactly what you want, and repeat them over and over. Or create affirming songs, and sing them over and over. This works well because when you sing an affirmation, you engage the power of the heart chakra as well. When you bring these two energy centers into alignment, you release one of the most powerful forces on Earth.

I had a client, a stockbroker, who sang, "Life is such a honey because I so easily make money." It wasn't exactly poetry, to be sure, but it worked. He did make money. Another client, carless and sick of public transportation, took my suggestion and on a whim began to sing, "I'm going far in my new car, car, car!" Six months later a good friend told her that he was leaving for a year abroad and asked her if she would like to car-sit his Camry while he was gone. She answered by singing, "Yes, yes, yes!"

Expression is the outlet for how we want our lives to be. Life doesn't just happen to us, although it may feel as though it does. The truth is we decide how our lives are going to be. It is one hundred percent up to us. We are that powerful. And the magic wand that makes it happen is our expression. This is such a simple and easy statement that it is hard to believe. And yet it is true. When we fully realize that we are spiritual creators, life does become our dream.

Write a positive affirmation that states who you wish to be and what you want to create.

_____

_____

_____

BALANCING YOUR EXPRESSION

When your expression is *slightly* imbalanced

- Greet others in a kind and positive manner.
- Make positive predictions throughout the day.
- Write thank-you letters.
- Leave a positive or funny message on someone's answering machine.
- Use a "New Word for the Day" calendar.
- Breathe before you speak.
- Breathe while listening.
- Practice saying what you want to say in advance.
- Sing in the shower.
- Drink plenty of flavorful hot teas.
- Wear something sky blue around your neck, such as a tie, necklace, or scarf.

When your expression is *moderately* imbalanced

- Every time you catch yourself saying something negative, immediately say, "Cancel! Cancel!"

- Count to ten before you speak—to one hundred if you are angry.

- Go someplace remote, and loudly scream, chant, or sing.

- Learn a new language.

- Write letters to those with whom you want to connect or come to closure.

- Say, "I am ___" and finish the sentence with what best reflects your heart's desire.

- Create and recite a positive slogan or mantra for yourself.

- Ask your Higher Self for guidance.

- Practice expressing yourself in an artistic way, such as drawing, writing, or dancing.

- Observe silence for ten minutes a day.

- Rent the movie *Gandhi* by Richard Attenborough.

- Respond to negativity with silence.

- Speak the truth for one day.

- Get a neck rub to "uncork" what may be bottled up.

- Sing a great new song at the top of your lungs in the car.

- Rather than waiting for the "right" moment, make an appointment to speak with someone with whom you feel the need to communicate or connect.

- Take off your tie, and open your collar.

When your expression is *seriously* imbalanced

- Take a public speaking course, join a speaking organization such as Toastmasters, or get a private speech coach.

- Scream into a pillow.

- Get a joke book, and memorize some good jokes. Then tell them regularly to those around you.

- Practice *aaaahs*: Every morning when you get out of bed, stretch and inhale. Then slowly exhale, letting out a nice, long, loud *"AAAAHHHHHHHHH!!!"* Do this two or three times to warm up your throat chakra and prepare you to express yourself fully in the day ahead.

- Make yourself laugh.

- Do your own intuitive reading.

- Do an intuitive reading for a friend.

- Observe silence for twenty minutes a day.

- Say yes to yourself every day.

- Take singing lessons.

- Speak to a professional counselor or therapist who specializes in expressing feelings, such as a Gestalt therapist.

- Listen to your intuition.

- Allow only healthy things to pass your lips (in either direction).

- Put a drop of your favorite essential oil on your skin at the base of your neck, where your throat chakra lies.

Remember, expression is

Speaking
Honesty
Laughter
Listening
Creativity
Telepathy
Rapport
Connection
Revealing
Expression
Truth

As your fifth chakra comes back into balance, don't be surprised if you find yourself feeling inspired with creative ideas of your own for keeping it that way. As you do, list them below.

_____

_____

_____

Sixth Chakra

Balanced Personal Vision

THE SIXTH CHAKRA, also known as the third eye, originates between the eyebrows and expands outward, governing the entire upper portion of the head, from the top of the forehead to the tip of the nose. This energy center focuses on our ability to see accurately in life. It encompasses our ability to analyze, think, reason, perceive, understand, discern, dream, imagine, and visualize. The upper octave of the sixth chakra is also the center for the psychic gift of clairvoyance, a French word meaning "clear sight." On the color spectrum, this chakra vibrates to a deep indigo blue, like a clear winter sky at midnight. When it is balanced, it is the center of personal inner vision. Its mission statement is: "I see. I understand. I imagine."

On a physiological level, this chakra governs the head, the eyes, all the sense organs, the brain, and the nervous system, and when imbalanced it may affect the health of these areas as well. Once we establish and balance our expression, we are then able to travel upward into this sixth center of energy and awaken our personal vision and begin to see the truth in the world.

The sixth chakra operates in conjunction with the pituitary gland and enhances our memory, our dream state, and our ability to learn intellectually and to understand the nature of the world around us. It also sharpens our ability to accurately review the past, which includes developing a good memory, and it helps us to envision a better future. On an energy level, this center influences our ability to see the world and ourselves without distortion and opens our eyes to beauty and art as essential food for the soul.

If your personal vision is imbalanced, you may suffer headaches, dizziness, eyestrain or weak vision, or have difficulty concentrating or focusing. On an emotional level, imbalanced personal vision may cause you to have problems conveying ideas or perceiving the ideas of others. It might also cause you to have delusions or paranoia, suffer from memory lapses, or fall into doomsday thinking. Other frequent personal vision problems are overintellectualizing, disconnecting with the more subtle nonphysical dimensions of life, and missing the point. A person whose personal vision is blocked may have great difficulty seeing others with an open mind and may tend to be controlling and perfectionistic, putting up a false front and emphasizing appearances over honest self-expression.

BALANCED PERSONAL VISION

When our personal vision is sharp and balanced, it awakens our ability to look at life with a creative and positive point of view, and it stimulates our thirst for knowledge and education in every possible way. The sixth chakra energy center invites our imagination to work with our reason, allowing us to recognize the true nature of all that we see, both physically and with our inner eye. When the third eye is fully balanced, we are able to see ourselves and others as energetically fluid spiritual beings; we have the power to create our reality using our imagination, freedom of choice, and insight.

Balanced personal vision is our headlight, so to speak, leading us out of the darkness of internal confusion and distortion and into a clear, thoughtful, and balanced world. It awakens our desire to look for the wonder and beauty in all things. It is the center from which we evaluate the conditions of our life, record our experiences, and activate our inspiration and direction, showing us our path and purpose. When it is balanced and open, our personal vision sharpens our attention and concentration skills. It also sparks our desire to seek accurate information rather than blindly accept secondhand opinions as fact.

This energy station stimulates our concern for all human beings and raises our sensitivity to injustice, indifference, ignorance, and all else that prevents people from living in dignity and safety. It activates us to reach for solutions to personal and world problems, and it bestows upon us intuitive flashes, thus paving the way for action. This is the center where creative genius is born. Not only does it accurately reveal the hidden nature of the difficulties we face, it also points us toward effective and long-lasting solutions.

LOOKING PAST APPEARANCES

Our center of personal vision is often referred to as our "internal movie screen," upon which we project our musings, imaginings, and dreams. It serves as the primary laboratory for our ideas, inventions, and perceptions. Here in our imagination, most of us determine how we are going to experience life. So much of what we experience is, in fact, an internal drama dictated by our imagination. As Mark Twain wrote, "I've experienced many terrible things in life, a few of which actually happened." When our sixth center is open and balanced, we pay close attention to the world around us and refrain from jumping to conclusions before learning all there is to know about any given situation or person. We come instead to understand intuitively that appearances can be misleading and that there is always more than meets the eye.

One of my clients, Donna, a flight attendant, told me a story that illustrates how our perception of a situation can be unexpectedly blown wide open. She was staying in Washington, D.C., on a layover and had to depart for her flight at five the next morning. As she boarded the hotel bus to the airport, a family of six immigrants followed behind her. The minute they got on, she was immediately overwhelmed by their disheveled appearance and body odor. Completely disgusted, she thought, "Stupid, dirty immigrants. Don't they know how to bathe?"

As they took their places on the bus, she covered her nose with her scarf, making no effort to hide her revulsion. She deliberately avoided any eye contact with them as a way of punishing them for offending her. As soon as they arrived at the airport, she jumped off the bus, her eyes throwing daggers at the entire group as she departed.

Once on the aircraft at her station by the front door, she was appalled to see this same family, smelling to high heaven, heading down the jetway and about to board her plane. She reached over to get the air freshener normally used for the lavatory and generously spritzed the air as they walked past her, again avoiding eye contact. Moments later, other flight attendants came up to complain about how the group smelled. "I know!" she said. "Aren't they disgusting? They should be thrown off the plane." She was relieved that at least she didn't have to be near them during the flight, as she was working in first class.

An hour into the flight, a crewmember came rushing up to first class and summoned her to the back, saying, "Hurry, a passenger just fainted! We need your help." She ran to the back of the aircraft and found that the passenger in trouble was one of the immigrants, a young man of about twenty. In an attempt to figure out what was wrong with him, she turned to the old woman next to him. For the first time, she looked directly at her and was overcome by the panic and fear in the old woman's eyes.

Hurriedly, through a series of gestures and words, Donna learned that they were a family traveling from Russia to Seattle. They had left the country with only the clothes on their backs and no money. Someone from their church group was supposed to meet them in Washington and look after them for a few days until they made the last leg of their journey. Unfortunately, that contact person never arrived. They were forced to sleep in the airport, and apparently they had had no food and virtually no sleep for days. No wonder the young man had collapsed.

Donna immediately gave the young man her own crew breakfast. As he came around, the old woman kissed her hands again and again, thanking her and apologizing for their state. "I know we smell bad." She gestured. "I'm sorry." As Donna looked into the faces of these poor people, her heart opened, and she was ashamed of herself for passing such harsh judgment against them only moments earlier.

Once they landed in St. Louis, Donna personally escorted them to their connecting flight so that she could ask the next flight crew to have more compassion for them than she had had. She first stopped at the snack bar along the way and bought them all hot dogs and Cokes. The minute she saw them off, she knew that she had just learned an important spiritual lesson. From that day forward, she vowed never again to judge anyone by appearance alone.

When your personal vision is open and balanced, your often-distorted perceptions and expectations of the world no longer hold you hostage. You begin to see beyond the physical and awaken a second sight called insight. When this aspect of seeing is in place, we begin to notice the similarities that human beings share rather than focus on our apparent differences. This opens the door to more tolerance, understanding, and compassion.

HOW BALANCED IS YOUR PERSONAL VISION?

	Yes	No	Sometimes
I pay attention to small details.	____	____	____
I notice what others overlook.	____	____	____
I get the "facts" before I draw conclusions.	____	____	____
I have vivid dreams.	____	____	____
I can easily visualize something in my mind's eye.	____	____	____
I have a good and accurate memory.	____	____	____
I am able to concentrate on something for a long period of time.	____	____	____

	Yes	No	Sometimes
I appreciate art and see it as essential in my life.	———	———	———
I refrain from judging people by appearances.	———	———	———
I can discern fact from fantasy.	———	———	———
I see into people and situations.	———	———	———
I have an open mind.	———	———	———
I am open to another's point of view.	———	———	———
I have a positive self-image.	———	———	———
I think things through before I make decisions.	———	———	———
I like to daydream.	———	———	———
I can easily imagine.	———	———	———
I seek accurate information.	———	———	———
I look for the hidden facets of life.	———	———	———
I like to problem-solve.	———	———	———

If you answered no to any one of these statements, your personal vision is somewhat blurred and imbalanced. If you answered no to two to five statements, your personal vision is slightly out of focus and imbalanced, and you should follow the suggestions for slight imbalances at the end of the chapter. If you answered no to six to nine statements, then your personal vision is somewhat blurred and moderately imbalanced, and you should follow the suggestions for adjusting moderate imbalances. If you answered no to ten or more statements, then your personal vision is seriously shut down. You should follow the suggestions for serious imbalances in order to expand your personal vision and see the beauty of the Universe.

IMAGINATION

Personal vision is also the realm of imagination. Here we are able to visualize and ultimately create the kind of experiences we want. When our personal vision is balanced, our imagination flows freely to create positive and inventive solutions for us. When we are faced with challenges or motivated by desires, it is our imagination that begins to activate solutions.

An assistant of mine, Nadia, shared with me her experience with the power of imagination. After the end of Communism in Ukraine, she, like thousands of others, found herself without a job. People were suddenly facing circumstances that required great resourcefulness. The harder it was for people to make money, the more creative they became in meeting their basic needs. People who had always worked for the state now started their own businesses, doing anything from knitting sweaters to growing food, driving taxis, opening restaurants, selling newspapers, and anything else they could think of. When they could no longer count on the state for their paycheck, it was amazing how quickly they were able to come up with other ways to earn money, legally or otherwise. Even though it was harder to live, day by day, the general atmosphere was more inspired, Nadia said, because the opportunities were now unlimited. Those with bright ideas did well. Those who surrendered their imaginations suffered. The way she describes it, "It brought out our best creative incentive. We didn't have the luxury to imagine we wouldn't succeed, because it was absolutely certain that if we didn't help ourselves, no one else would."

This is the genius of personal vision. It takes us from what we are experiencing today and shows us how to create an even better tomorrow. A teacher of mine once said, "You cannot create what you cannot imagine. Conversely, you always create what you do imagine."

What do you imagine most in your life?

_____

_____

When faced with a problem, do you use your imagination to find solutions, or do you allow your imagination to "run away with you," conjuring up worst-case scenarios?

_____

_____

Was anyone in your family particularly imaginative when you were young?

_____

_____

Did anyone ever capture your imagination when you were young?

_____

_____

IMAGINE THROUGH EVERY SENSE

Some of my students and clients complain that they have difficulty imagining in images. "I never imagine in pictures," one woman told me at my last intuition workshop. "Something must be wrong with me. Everyone else seems to be having the equivalent of a Cecil B. DeMille movie going on in their minds, and all I see is a blank gray screen."

To this, I have to say several things. First, I believe that the best imaginings are a synthesis of all the senses; second, we do not all naturally imagine in pictures. Some of us imagine in feelings, and some of us imagine in thoughts. The first thing to do is to pinpoint how you do imagine or experience your inner life. Once you identify your own style, try to boost your imagination by integrating your other senses into it—a process I first introduced in my book *Your Heart's Desire*.

If you want to use your imagination to create a new job, start by imagining the desired job through each sense, one at a time. Begin with what your ideal job sounds like. What sounds would be present at your workplace? Try voicing out loud the kinds of conversations you would have with colleagues. What clothes would you wear? Then move on to your work environment. If, for example, you want to be a writer, would you use a computer or a pen? Would you sit at a desk or work at a table? Bring your focus to the tactile feelings of a keyboard or a beautiful pen. What hours would you work? Then ask yourself how the environment would smell. For instance, if your ideal job is in an office, you might want to imagine a flower stall nearby, supplying you with a steady supply of flowers for your desk. Perhaps there are windows that open to greenery outside. You can even try imagining how your desired work atmosphere would taste. Perhaps you'll have a freshly brewed cup of coffee from the office lunchroom or eat sushi from a nearby Japanese restaurant. Remember, imagination is a muscle that needs to be exercised, and these sorts of musings are how we strengthen it.

Finally, after running through all of those musings, imagine not only how your ideal work environment would look but how you would look in that environment and how looking that way would make you feel. If you do not think in pictures, look through magazines for pictures of your desired outcome and exercise your personal vision.

When I was talking to Lucia Cappachione, the author of *The Power of Your Other Hand,* about her beautiful house in central California, I asked her how she had found such an exquisite location and created such a marvelous house to live in. She told me that she began by collecting photos of exactly the kind of house she wanted and made a scrapbook of these images. Every photo she collected served to strengthen her idea of what she was looking for. Only two short months after she began her scrapbook, she found the exact counterpart to the house in her photos. She lives there to this day.

Another fabulous way to strengthen your personal vision is to do imagining gymnastics. For example, whenever you have a few extra minutes, imagine things in your mind's eye. You can start by imagining scenes that are very familiar, such as your bedroom or your workplace. Notice as many details as possible. Or you can imagine being in your car. Notice everything in it. After a while, you can begin imagining more challenging scenes, such as a yellow canary outside your window or a steaming bowl of pasta heaped high on a plate waiting to be served to you. Remember to use all of your senses as you do these exercises. Finally, work up to imagining those desires you want to create.

You can also strengthen your imagination by leaving the beaten track once in a while and visiting an unusual or unfamiliar place, one that requires you to pay absolute attention to all the details. For example, go to a new city for a weekend, see a foreign film, or go to the theater to see a play. It is especially exciting to do this exercise with people you know very well. I once decided to notice something new about Patrick, my husband of seventeen years, and discovered that he has a small bump on the back of his leg. I had never noticed it before, even though it is quite pronounced. When I found it, I assumed it had just appeared, but Patrick assured me that it was from an accident in college and had been there ever since. Though incidental, this discovery put me on notice to pay closer attention to things and people. After all, complacency in awareness radically diminishes our creativity and our perception of what is going on all around us.

What is your favorite way to imagine your heart's desire? Is it in pictures, sounds, daydreams, writing?

_____

_____

Have you ever successfully imagined something into being? How did you imagine it?

_____

_____

_____

SELF-IMAGE

Our sixth chakra governs our self-image; it is here that we form ideas about who we are and how we should present ourselves to the world. It usually reflects the persona formed by the expectations and beliefs of our primary caretakers in our early childhood.

I have a client, Jason, who has exceptional talents in photography, painting, and scenic design. He has a well-developed inner eye and continually surprises me with the depth and beauty of his artwork. And yet due to his confused self-image, Jason does not see himself as an artist and spends his days in a warehouse job that leaves him feeling quite depressed and frustrated. He grew up in a working-class family in Kentucky, with parents who did not appreciate his natural gifts and considered art a waste of time. In fact, his macho father called him a "sissy" and often asked him when he was going to stop "doing all that girly stuff," as he referred to Jason's projects, and become "a real man."

These negative messages about creative expression confused Jason, and he became ashamed of his gifts. In an effort to win his father's love and approval, he took up construction work and became a building supply warehouse foreman. He didn't abandon his artistic nature altogether, but whenever he did engage in some creative project like painting a landscape or taking a photograph, he felt as though it were costing him his manhood. This robbed him of any joy in this work.

Because Jason was presenting a self to the world that was neither genuine nor accessible, he found himself isolated and lonely. He couldn't relate to the macho characters he worked with and was cut off from any kinship with creative or artistic people. He was a morose loner who never let anyone into his life for fear that they would discover the truth about him—that he was a "sissy"—and do what his own family had done: reject him.

Jason's conflict was deep and required healing by skilled spiritual caretakers. I suggested that he begin by reading *The Artist's Way* by my dear friend Julia Cameron as a way to reclaim his natural self, as well as join a men's mentoring group to do repair work on his relationship with his father. Jason's work in reclaiming his true and authentic self was difficult and took place gradually over a number of years. But because he was so unhappy living a false life, he was persistent and eventually came to reclaim his genuine spirit. Today, at the age of forty-one, he paints at night and works during the day part time as a director for a local theater group. He also gives time to other distraught men at the same mentoring center that helped him reclaim his identity.

Jason's problem is not unique. In fact, it is probably the most common problem I encounter in my work as an intuitive and spiritual healer. As children, we are dependent on our caretakers not only for our physical well-being but also for affection and psychic safety. If we are told that in order to be loved, we must be other than ourselves, we do so, but at a grave cost. Boys may be tormented with macho messages about masculinity and forced to reject their creative and sensitive natures along the way. Girls are told their self-worth is dependent not on their creativity and mental capacities but on their bodies, and on behaving in socially dictated ways, such as being accommodating or "nice." Part of our progress in the new millennium will be the collective rejection of these dictates that steal away our true identities and our capacity to contribute fully in the world.

If you are struggling with your self-image, take heart. I can assure you that you are not alone. Reclaiming the authentic self can be challenging and is rarely achieved without the support and guidance of those who have walked the journey before you. Be open to asking for help along the way. Seek out teachers, counselors, healers, and companions. As our planet moves toward greater understanding, spiritual healers are becoming increasingly available. If healing your self-image is your desire, focus on your sixth chakra, and open your eyes to opportunity. Help is all around you, if you only start to look.

Describe yourself as you see yourself today.

_____

_____

Describe how others see you.

_____

_____

Describe your ideal self. What is the self that you want to be?

_____

_____

How far are you from being the "you" that you want to be?

_____

_____

TRY THIS!

Present Yourself as a Work of Art
Every morning take the time to make yourself look and feel beautiful. Be considerate of those who will look at you, and give them a wonderful treat by sharing with them your most attractive self. Style your hair.

Apply your makeup carefully if you wear it. Groom your mustache. Scrub your fingernails. Wear colors that are flattering. Choose a beautiful outfit or tie, and be creative. Put on a hat for a change, as my friend Nancy does when she wants to be beautiful. She calls it "hat-titude"! If you are a man, wear a bow tie or bolo tie instead of an ordinary one, and throw on a little aftershave. Not only will you be making a small but meaningful contribution to the beautification of the planet, but people who take the time to look their best are treated better than those who don't.

 ## TRY THIS!

Be a Model for a Day

Ask a friend to join you in playing "model" for a day. Bring cameras and several rolls of film, and drive all over town together finding interesting locations where you can photograph each other. Use this as an opportunity to act as both photographer and actor, and invite all of your unexpressed selves to come out and play. This remedy is terrific fun, and you may be surprised at how creative and photogenic you are.

SEEKING THE BEAUTIFUL

One of the most important functions of our personal vision is to direct our awareness to the beauty that surrounds us. It is all too easy to have our perspective diminished by others, including parents, teachers, and the media, leaving us with the impression that the world is less than the magnificent place that it is. The general consensus tends to slide to the lowest common denominator, emphasizing and at times exaggerating the worst and literally blinding us to all that is beautiful and soul enriching in life.

A Hawaiian healer once told me that one of the worst soul diseases a person can have is something the Hawaiians call "stink eye." This is the condition of seeing the world and the people in it through the negative viewpoint of your own misery. "If you have stink-eye, you miss everything," the healer said, laughing. Looking at his radiantly beautiful face, I believed him.

We can actively look for the beauty in all circumstances, no matter how challenging. When I suggested this to a spiritually ambitious client, Eileen, who was struggling with a terribly disabling case of rheumatoid arthritis, she cried, "But look at my gnarled fingers! I want to have a spiritual viewpoint, but how can I ever see my grotesque hands as beautiful! I hate them!"

Appreciative of her despair and her chronic pain, I suggested that perhaps there was more to notice and observe than just her crippled hands. "Let's explore together the journey that has attended your illness," I said. "Perhaps it isn't your hands specifically that offer the gift of beauty. Perhaps there is something hidden behind them that may carry a gift."

As I questioned her about her life before and after her disease, I heard her story. An only child, unmarried, never having been in a committed relationship, she told me that she was the owner of a successful boutique and painted as a hobby. Until she was stricken with her illness, she had been a very independent woman who fully supported herself "in every sense of the word," as she emphasized. She didn't rely on anyone, didn't answer to anyone, and was free to do exactly what she wanted without interference.

As a child, she had been the constant companion of her single mother, who became stricken with multiple sclerosis when Eileen was eleven. She was her "mother's brave little girl" and was praised for her independence, because as her mother constantly emphasized, "needing to depend upon someone is the worst!" Being the one depended upon, Eileen secretly agreed. "So I created a life that guaranteed that I would never be in her position. Never!" said Eileen proudly, as she summarized her life. "And now this"—she lifted her gnarled fingers—"has screwed everything up!"

"Were you happy before you became ill?" I asked her. "Of course," she answered automatically. "Wouldn't you be?"

"Hm. Let me think," I said. "Probably not. That much independence sounds lonely. I think I'd personally long to reach out for some support."

Eileen listened for a minute, and then tears welled up in her eyes.

"Well, if I really tell the truth, I guess I have been lonely. Very lonely. But reaching out wasn't the style in my family. I never considered it."

"How have things changed since your illness began?" I questioned further.

"That's a good question," she said. "Well, I guess the first thing that changed is that I had to hire someone to help at the boutique. I didn't want to because of the costs, but surprisingly, I actually like the gal, and it has made work a lot more fun. Even though I worry, it seems like the bills get paid, although I'm not sure how. I have also begun a spiritual journey to try and heal my health, and although my hands are still deteriorating, I have to admit I've met some incredible people. Perhaps even more important, I now feel much closer to God. I guess I don't feel as alone as I did before this all began."

"So would you say that your crippled hands have caused you to see things differently and reach out after all?" I suggested. "Yes," she said, as if shocked by the revelation. "Perhaps, then, that's the beauty of this disease," I said. "Perhaps it was your body's way of giving you the opportunity to receive the love and support that we all need and deserve in life. Given your history, I wonder if you would have accepted it any other way."

What circumstances or situations in your life appear to be the most difficult or cause you the most sorrow?

_____

_____

Are there any aspects to this situation that you have overlooked that may help you see it differently?

_____

_____

What negative images plague you the most?

_____

_____

What beautiful images soothe your spirit the most?

_____

_____

Are you stuck in a persona that limits you, such as "good girl," "brave man," or "hard worker"?

_____

_____

☼ TRY THIS!

Look for the Silver Lining

Every time you find yourself in an upsetting situation, practice seeking the silver lining. In other words, actively look for the gifts that come disguised in loss, frustration, and disappointment. This ritual will offset any tendency to feel like a victim and give away your power. It will keep your imagination oriented toward seeing your opportunities to grow and evolve as a spiritual being. Create a "silver linings" journal specifically for recording new perspectives, and make an entry once a day. Even if you're not convinced at the beginning, the very act of doing this will shift your attitude; you'll be looking for the gifts in your life instead of dwelling on the problems. I have found in doing this that it may be weeks, months, or even years before I can return to my journal and acknowledge the gifts I've received, but never have I had an experience that didn't eventually bring me great gifts.

SEEING THE WHOLE PICTURE

One of the benefits of having balanced personal vision is the ability to accurately assess our situation before we make any decisions. After all, if we can't accurately assess our conditions, we cannot effectively choose or correct them. This means being able to see good and bad before drawing conclusions, avoiding both sentimental enthusiasm and pessimistic avoidance. A balanced sixth chakra lets us be open minded and unbiased, willing to see all aspects and learn whatever we can before we decide what to do.

Balanced personal vision serves as a bridge between the left, rational, thinking brain and the right, intuitive, feeling brain. Creating this whole-brained approach to life supports our ability to place our full attention on what we want to create, accurately observe where we are at the moment, and then objectively look for the most direct path from here to there.

Several years ago Patrick and I decided it was time to buy our first house. I was eager to create our "dream home," and in my right-brained enthusiasm, every house that we saw in our price range looked perfect—I wanted to buy it right away! I was sure that no matter what we purchased, I would be able to transform it into a "house beautiful" in no time. Patrick, on the other hand, ignored the aesthetic qualities of each house and, in his left-brained approach to life, headed immediately for the basement, where he could examine the wiring, the gas line, and the foundation for any signs of past flooding. He wasn't concerned with how the house looked so much as how it was built and what condition it was in.

Our perspectives clashed considerably. Every time I found the ideal house, with charming wood paneling, fine location, or generous room sizes, Patrick saw only a handyman's nightmare, with haphazard wiring, a basement that obviously flooded, and rotten floor joists. After many discussions in which I perceived him to be completely negative and he perceived me to be totally unrealistic, we eventually came to appreciate the other's point of view. Because we had started the search so far apart in our visions, this effort required a real workout for our sixth chakras. Finally, we found a house that was perfect from both of our perspectives: it was charming, required work, but wasn't beyond our ability to fix. We again learned the importance of having a clear vision of our desires while acknowledging what we were working with in the moment. It's important not to let appearances in the moment discourage you, but rather to let them serve as a yardstick for your beginning point. In our case, we could have a "house beautiful," but first we had to be sure it was fundamentally sound.

List the three most positive attributes of your life today.

_____

_____

_____

List the three most negative aspects of your life today.

_____

_____

_____

List your three best traits.

_____

_____

_____

List your three greatest weaknesses.

_____

_____

_____

Have you ever been accused of being a Pollyanna? Are you?

_____

Have you ever been accused of being too negative or a "downer"? Are you?

_____

TRY THIS!

What Did You See?
See a movie or a play with someone, and afterward describe your experience as you saw it. Did the two of you have the same experience?

LOOK ON THE BRIGHT SIDE
Our personal vision acts as a bridge between our interior world and the outer world. When it is open and balanced, it helps us bridge the gap between dreams and reality. It shows us how to shape our hopes to adapt to the physical reality we must work in, and it shows us how to shape the real world to make our dreams come true. This center, when operating in optimum flow, blends our capacity to learn with our capacity to create. It allows us to intellectually grasp a situation and imaginatively construct an ideal.

Our personal vision also governs our ability to have a positive outlook on life—to see opportunity in every roadblock and take life's curve-balls as challenges rather than affronts. People who have a balanced sixth chakra have an optimistic, resourceful point of view. They endlessly seek ways to achieve their dreams and to see obstacles as the sport of life, in which the name of the game is overcoming hurdles with grace.

A person with balanced personal vision looks ahead, noticing where he can be creative, where there are openings, and where he can make connections that bring about good for all concerned. These are not nec-essarily people who attract attention to themselves, either.

I had a client in Chicago who, along with thirty-five other employees, had just been downsized from her corporate job of twenty years. While most of her colleagues were in a state of panic over the situation, she decided that it was simply the Universe's way of telling her that it had other plans for her. "I'm not going to worry about it," she said. "I'm going to take a vacation instead and worry about it later. Something bet-ter will show up, and I'm going to relax until it does." Everyone she knew criticized her for her laissez-faire attitude and told her she was being irresponsible in not immediately looking for another job.

"I will when I'm ready," she said, "but for right now, I'm going to visit Colorado, where I've always wanted to go. I'll trust that the Uni-verse will show me where to go after my trip!" She booked a ticket and left the same day she cleared out her desk. Having no particular reason to get back to Chicago, she allowed herself several weeks to explore the Rockies. One day she was sitting in a coffee shop in Aspen next to a gen-tleman who was friendly and eager to talk. She told him she had recently lost her job and was traveling around deciding what she wanted to do next. Then she commented that she loved Colorado so much that she wished she could find interesting work there. "What kind of work are you interested in?" he asked.

"Oh, I don't know," my client replied. "I'm in the mood for a real change. To tell the truth, I'd love to be outside running around and not stuck behind a desk." As they continued to chat, she discovered that he was a high-powered realtor, with developments all over the country. He lived part time in Aspen and spent the rest of his time in Connecticut or London. As they continued to talk, he told her that he was looking for someone to manage his estate in Aspen, and on a whim he offered her the job. All she had to do was live in the house and host the endless stream of guests who frequented his estate. Surprising herself, she accepted the job on the spot. When she returned to Chicago to pack her things, her friends and family couldn't believe her good fortune, or the fact that she was willing to make such a radical shift in her life. "It doesn't make sense to them that I would make such a big move at my age," she said, "but the way I see it, why not? It's exactly the life I had always secretly dreamed of."

TRY THIS!

Star in Your Own Movie

Try looking at your life as if it were a movie. What kind of movie would it be? Is your life a romance, a comedy, a drama, an art film, or a farce? If you were to choose a famous actor to play you, who would it be? Who else would star in your movie as supporting cast? As your mother? As your partner? Where would the great movie of your life be filmed? What era? What would your character do next? Where would your character go next? What would be your character's greatest quality? Practicing this ritual helps you step away from your life's dramas and get perspective; it can even help you laugh at yourself, which will have a powerful, perspective-shifting effect.

LINEAR VIEW

One sign of a distorted inner vision is the tendency to be overly intellectual. When we focus exclusively on the physical world, we end up ignoring the more subtle complexities of the human experience. People who suffer from this distortion tend to be controlling and perfectionist in their thinking, making life for them and those around them tense and unpleasant.

One of my clients, Gina, spent most of her twenties and thirties going to school, collecting graduate degrees and proving to herself and others that she was a smart person. She was also a controlling and self-righteous person who believed that her academic credentials made her right at all times. Her colleagues found her obnoxious; she had no sense of humor and acted as if the rest of the human race were just barely tolerable. Though she would get hired for top positions, she was ultimately fired or quit from each one because of her arrogance and her inability to cooperate with others.

Desperate after being fired for the fourth time, she came to see me, although she still considered what I do "a joke." I saw that she had a severely distorted personal vision and had fallen completely out of touch with the sensitive, intuitive side of the human experience. She had reduced life to facts, data, and information and tried to make everyone else do the same.

I explained to Gina, in terms I thought she could relate to, that she had lost touch with her right brain—her feeling, intuitive self—and that it was her views that were lopsided, not the views of every single person she ever worked with, as she believed. Though she heard the words, the message was more than she could absorb with her linear perspective. What seemed even more outrageous to her was the notion that she was causing her own difficulties, a concept that conflicted with her carefully constructed persona. So she laughed at me and said, "I thought you were going to explain why they were all so stupid! This psychobabble doesn't help me at all." And she left.

I didn't see her again for over three years. After she left me, she was hired by another firm and was eventually fired after a male coworker filed a sex-discrimination lawsuit against her for rude comments. Finally scared, she made another appointment with me. This time she was more open to hearing what I had to say. I explained that her problems were not due to her being such a bad person or even a failure. Rather, they were due to her inability to see the entire picture. Because she believed that life could be lived on strictly intellectual terms, she was the energetic equivalent of a bull in a china shop in her interactions with other people. In truth, she was psychically handicapped and would remain so until she reintegrated the more sensitive side of her perception into her reality.

It was time for Gina to go back to the classroom and learn about aspects of life she had missed the first time. And the classrooms she needed to visit weren't in universities. I suggested that she attend a drawing class to learn better how to perceive others. I also gave her a catalog of classes offered at the local spiritual center on subtle energy work, such as Reiki, a universal healing mode. I encouraged her to explore and experience the world of energy. "Gina," I said, "the problem with your world is that what you see and know is true but incomplete. And until you have the whole picture, the parts you have are misleading."

Gina's repeated failures to achieve success had been humiliating to her, but her setbacks paved the way for a more open mind. She began to gain some insight into the world of others, a whole new arena of discovery, and in doing so she began the important work of balancing her personal vision. Finally, because some habits die hard, she also wisely decided to leave the corporate world and became self-employed.

Having a distorted or incomplete view of life can put even the most educated person at a great disadvantage. My teachers always taught me that the sign of a well-educated person is the ability to see not only what is obvious, but what is hidden as well. The best way to balance your personal vision is to recognize what is hidden, which is that we are all spiritual beings. Becoming disconnected from this part of our nature is the psychic equivalent of having one of our limbs amputated. You can survive this devastating experience but not without great cost to your spirit.

In what area of your life do you have the most difficulty seeing the bigger picture?

_____

_____

Do you have any recurring difficulties, such as the same problem with different people or in different places?

_____

_____

Do you tend to focus on the physical aspects or the spiritual components of a problem?

_____

_____

Have you ever been accused of being narrow minded? Are you?

_____

Do you often see others as wrong and yourself as the victim?

_____

Can you allow yourself to see another's point of view?

_____

Do you?

_____

DREAMS

One domain of personal vision is the dream world. This is where our spirit works to reveal to us facets of our unconscious, our emotions, and our higher knowing. Our dream world is the place where our souls reveal messages to us, helping us sort out the complexities of day-to-day life.

There are many ways to connect to your dream world and the first is to make a point of paying attention to your dreams. It helps enormously to keep a dream journal next to your bed and to train yourself to record your dreams first thing every morning or even during the night if your dream rouses you. Keeping a dream journal may seem like a chore in the beginning, but the effort is well worth it, for it will enable you to get in touch with lost parts of your nature and other dimensions of consciousness, as well as spirit travel.

Another way to reclaim your dreams is to suggest to yourself before you go to bed that you will remember them. What has worked for me is the following technique. I take a drink of water just before bed, and as I drink, I say to myself, "I will remember my dreams the minute I take a sip of water in the morning." Then in the morning, as soon as I wake up, I take another drink from the same glass of water. Just as I programmed my subconscious mind to do, I remember my dream.

You can also stimulate your personal vision by daydreaming once in a while. Our ability to visualize can be developed like a muscle. The more we use these creative parts of our minds, the stronger they become. Daydreaming invites your spirit to bring new ideas and creative solutions into your conscious awareness. It creates an opportunity for your spirit to communicate with you and to make you aware of options you may never have considered before. Daydreaming allows you to live your unlived life. If you do it often enough, these experiences will move from the unconscious into your actual world. The more you visualize something, the less frightening or stressful it will be in reality.

Daydreams and night dreams both take us out of the subjective, ego-based realm of personality and connect us to our Universal Self. Dreams serve to strengthen our ability to understand others and ourselves in the deepest possible way. Many dream experts have written books that are well worth reading. Some of my favorite authors are Patricia Garfield, who wrote *Creative Dreaming,* and Robert Johnson, who wrote *Inner Work* and *Lucid Dreaming.* Taking a dream class at the local community college or spiritual center in your town can also be valuable. Finally, it helps to find someone to share your dreams with. With a little attention, you may come to see a pattern in your dream symbols and decipher an entire dream language for yourself.

Do you remember your dreams?

Do you pay attention to your dreams?

_____

Do you like to daydream? About what?

_____

_____

Do you ever write down your dreams or keep a dream journal?

_____

Do you share your dreams or daydreams with anyone? Who?

_____

Do you have recurring dreams? What do you think these dreams are trying to convey?

_____

_____

CLAIRVOYANCE

One of the most extraordinary benefits of fully awakened personal vision is clairvoyant sight, which includes the ability to see auras, chakras, and even probable future events. Clients and students frequently ask me if I really believe they will be able to see these things for themselves. Not only do I believe that people can develop these clairvoyant qualities, I think that they are completely natural to us. As more people begin to perceive themselves as spiritual beings, these abilities will become more and more commonplace.

Clairvoyance is not the bizarre and otherworldly phenomenon that Hollywood has made it out to be. It is the natural consequence of the profound perspective that comes with a highly developed and balanced sixth chakra. When we remove the filters of bias and subjectivity from our eyes, we begin to awaken our clairvoyant capacities. If we pay attention to the world around us, notice subtle energies, try to see the truth, refrain from judging others, and remember that there is more than meets the eye, then it is only natural that we will become clairvoyant. This is because the spiritual gift of clairvoyance is simply the ability to see the truth. No hocus-pocus or contrivance is involved. You do not have to attend special classes or follow any crazy spiritual belief system to be clairvoyant. All it requires is a desire on your part to see the most accurate picture of our magnificent world. Wanting to see the true nature of life, free of distortion, will awaken your highest spiritual capacities and show you the same hidden realities that holy men and women have perceived for centuries.

I personally believe that as we move into the new millennium and reclaim our spiritual heritage, clairvoyance, as well as our other spiritual senses, will fully awaken in us naturally. I believe that this is not only possible, but that as we usher in the age of peace, it is part of the Divine plan.

Have you ever had a premonition? About what?

_____

_____

_____

Have you ever had a precognitive dream?

_____

_____

Have you ever seen an aura or imagined that you had?

_____

Can you see the beauty and wonder of your magnificent soul?

_____

Can you see the Divine in all things and people?

_____

BALANCING PERSONAL VISION

When you are *slightly* imbalanced

- Write a positive affirmation on your bathroom mirror, such as "Hello, Beautiful!" or "You look marvelous!"

- Place a beautiful photo or piece of art in your workplace.

- Visit a beautiful spot, and have a picnic.

- Play memory games.

- Attend an art opening at a local gallery.

- Plant flowers.

- Invent a recipe and make it. Then serve it on your best china.

- Eat lunch at a glamorous restaurant with a favorite friend.

- If you are a woman, do your makeup completely differently. Try Egyptian kohl-lined eyes, gold eye shadow, or dramatic lip-liner. If you are a man, get a dramatic new haircut or flattering new eyeglasses or colored contact lenses.

- Put up a bulletin board for your favorite photographs.

- List the three most beautiful things you saw today.

- Get some pet birds.

- Ask a trusted and loving friend to be your "flattery friend" for a day and to describe all your wonderful qualities.

- Create an inspirational screen-saver on your computer screen.

- Get an indigo blue shirt or scarf.

When you are *moderately* imbalanced

- Look into the mirror and into your own eyes, and say: "Mirror, mirror on the wall, who's the fairest of them all? Me! That's who!"

- Take up photography.

- Take an architectural tour of your city.

- Put a fun and wild temporary tattoo in a secret place on your body (or a loved one's body).

- Finger-paint with your kids, and hang your masterpiece up.

- Play the *I Spy* 3D magic eye book series.

- Clean up your house.

- Make your own greeting cards.

- Rent the movie *Dreams* by Akira Kurosawa or *Buena Vista Social Club* by Wim Wenders

- Buy an inspirational piece of art.

- When eating at home, present your food in the most beautiful way on your plate, complete with garnish.

- Put attractive photos, ads, or cartoons up on the refrigerator.

- Redecorate your living room.

- Make your own flower arrangement.

- Design your own tarot cards.

- Tell someone how much you love him or her and why. Describe all their beautiful qualities.

- Get rid of all your ugly and unflattering clothes.

- Comb your hair, put on makeup, and dress your best, even if you are not going anywhere special.

- Have a professional photo taken of yourself.

- Look for some new detail that you have never noticed before in everyone you know.

- Get a color analysis at your local department-store cosmetic counter, or read *Color Me Beautiful* by Carole Jackson.

When you are *seriously* imbalanced

- Take a dream class at the local university.

- Set up an aquarium with tropical fish.

- Go on a three-day judgment fast of yourself and others.

- Take a watercolor or drawing class.

- Visit an art gallery.

- Keep a "silver linings" journal of experiences that turned out better than they appeared.

- Practice visualizing having a beautiful day in detail before you get out of bed.

- Create a meditation garden or corner in your home.

- Feng shui your home to create a balanced atmosphere.

- Clean up your neighborhood.

- Join a film club.

- Every time you look into a mirror, smile!

- Visualize succeeding at the things you want to do in life.

- Look for God in everyone and everything.

Remember, inner vision is

Perception
Discernment
Imagination
Dreams
Memory
Daydreams
Clairvoyance
Insight
Open-mindedness
Visualization
Reason
Thinking
Viewpoint
Invention

As you regain balance in your sixth chakra, your spirit will inspire you to create remedies for maintaining this balance on your own. Write down all your ideas in the space below.

_____

_____

_____

_____

_____

Seventh Chakra

Your Crowning Glory

THE SEVENTH CHAKRA, also known as the crown chakra, and as the thousand-petal lotus for its fabled number of facets, is located at the highest point of the body, on the top of the head. It is the center for our highest spiritual consciousness and personal expression. When awakened and balanced, this energy station connects us to our source of life, God, and opens our way to becoming a bearer of light to the world. The seventh chakra transcends all our other senses and allows us to experience God and the goodness of the Universe directly. On the color spectrum, it vibrates energetically to the color violet, fading into white at the edges. In contrast to the fourth chakra ("I love"), the fifth ("I hear"), and the sixth ("I see"), the seventh chakra's mission statement is simply "I know."

Our crown center focuses our attention on the spiritual meaning of life and begins to erase the imagined demarcation between what is spiritual and what is not. Once we establish balance in our personal vision, we are able to move energetically upward to the crown chakra, where we begin to merge with our Source.

When our crown is open, we awaken to the understanding that all things are made out of the same universal mind stuff and that in fact everything is spiritual. This center clears away the illusion that we are anything less than Divine children, spiritual heirs to the kingdom of Heaven.

On a physiological level, the crown chakra is connected to the brain stem, the spinal cord, the nervous system, and the pineal gland, located in the brain, and when imbalanced it may affect the health of these areas as well. Life-threatening diseases such as ALS or AIDS also fall under the domain of the crown chakra, as they are connected to one's soul growth in this lifetime. This energy station allows you to be calm, deeply at ease, fully aware, and yet low key and understated. In this aware frame of mind, you will know without a doubt that all forms of life are intimately connected to one another and that we are indeed one body, one spiritual family on Earth.

When your crown opens, it actually radiates energy above your head, sending out a violet-white glow that can be seen as a radiant light around your face. In religious art, an opened crown center is shown as a beautiful golden halo surrounding the head.

When your crown is open and balanced, you will develop a gentle and compassionate nature, free from all anxiety or concern for your own safety or personal well-being. Instead, you will move into a state of absolute faith that the Universe is well aware of all that you need and is even better able to bring it to you than you are. All concerns for personal effort transform into absolute faith that every genuine soulful need will be felt and, whether or not you are conscious of it, will be fulfilled by the Divine plan with grace and ease. This inner wisdom activates your capacity to express benevolence for your fellow humans without regard for what is in it for you.

The crown chakra does not become imbalanced. Rather it is either open, opening, or closed; even when it is only partially open, it is still balanced. The most obvious indication of a closed crown center is an absolute lack of faith. This includes having no faith in God, no faith in the order and wisdom of the Universe, and at worst, no faith in life itself; this condition is what is meant by the phrase a "dark night of the soul."

Awakening the crown chakra is the natural result of balancing your six other energy centers. Sometimes, however, it may open spontaneously in a reaction to a crisis or as a result of a deep and profound desire to know God. Opening the crown energy is a graceful maturing process that is the by-product of coming to understand our spiritual nature. Though to some it may seem as though they will never experience the awesome tranquillity of the awakened crown center, it is a natural part of our spiritual anatomy, and living the rest of our life in balance will naturally open it. There is no need to worry and no way to manipulate your crown into expansion. Like a planted tree, if you water the roots, the branches will bear fruit.

FAITH

When the crown center opens, we transcend the intellect and enter into the realm of faith. This understanding bypasses all need to justify or even understand the workings of the Universe. With an open crown, we shift into an awareness of Spirit that allows us to merge with our Source and become one with the Universe, as opposed to being an outsider looking on. Such activation can come from prayer and meditation, from spontaneous and life-changing experiences, or simply from a profound desire to know God, the Creator, and to surrender to Divine will for direction.

This energy center is the gateway to intimacy with our Creator. If the first chakra is the root that connects us to our Mother Earth, the seventh chakra connects us to our father, Divine Spirit. When we connect to both the first and seventh chakras, we complete the circuitry that channels our support for body, mind, and soul.

I spoke with a man, Sam, who told me the story about the opening of his crown chakra. He and his wife, Linda, had struggled with infertility treatments with no success. They were at their wit's end, completely demoralized by their unsuccessful and costly attempts to conceive a child. Their marriage hung by a thread as they fought to preserve the remnants of their shattered self-esteem. One day the thought of adoption planted itself in Sam's heart, and he instantly resolved that this was the Divine plan for them. Believing him, Linda agreed.

Surrendering completely to this directive, they made inquiries that led them to an attorney who represented children from Vietnam. As they made arrangements to go with him to get a baby, both Sam and Linda had terrible second thoughts about working with this man. But because they had invested so much time and money in the project, they forged ahead.

Once in Vietnam, they began getting confusing information from this attorney, and they soon realized he didn't have any connections there. His whole business was a sham. Both Sam and Linda were on the brink of nervous collapse, when Sam had a sudden, almost compulsive urge to call home and speak with the director of an adoption agency in Texas, whom he had contacted earlier. This instinct made no sense, but it was the kind of message that felt right, and so he followed it. After numerous tries, he finally succeeded in getting through. Though it was nine at night in Texas, someone working there overtime answered the phone. Sam explained their plight, and the man said, "Well, you're in luck. As it turns out, the agency director is in Beijing, and you can call him there." One call led to the next, and finally Sam succeeded in connecting with the director. Sam explained to him what had happened. He also told him that the anguish they were going through was almost too much to bear. "I don't even know why I'm calling," Sam said, "except that in my deepest prayer, something directed me to do so."

Apparently it was the right thing to do. Less than an hour after this phone call, the agency's Vietnam facilitator picked them up, and after a six-hour car trip, they were ushered into an orphanage. Once they were inside the building, Sam became dizzy and had to sit down. Perhaps it was the ordeal of travel, or the emotion of their finally being on the threshold of their greatest dream, but before he could meet with anyone, he absolutely had to rest and compose himself for a moment.

One of the women who ran the orphanage led Sam to a quiet darkened room where there were just a few sleeping babies in cribs. As he sat, an overwhelming peace flooded through his body. Seconds later, a tiny baby in one of the cribs started to fuss. He walked over and picked her up, and the minute he did, she quieted down. A few minutes later, Linda followed him into the room, and as she entered, she saw him holding the baby girl. She immediately knew it was to be their baby. Just as she entered, another baby, a five- or six-month-old boy, was waking up. She walked over to pick him up, and in that instant she knew that he too was to be part of their family. Miraculously, neither child was spoken for, and so the arrangements were made to allow Sam and Linda to take these two beautiful babies home. It was as if these children had called Sam and Linda from out of the ether to come and get them. They could only be humbly grateful that the Universe had chosen them to be parents.

Sam and Linda's experience illustrates the way of the seventh chakra, the way of faith. All along their intellects challenged them, their emotions fought them, and even their bodies worked against them. But something greater than all these forces led them on this journey to success. When I asked Sam what kept them moving forward on this unlikely and at times torturous journey, his answer was simply, "Prayer and faith. It was as if a higher force were running the show all along. This experience taught both Linda and me, without a doubt, that there is a higher intelligence operating in our lives at all times. I am only grateful that we didn't interfere with it."

I've known people with this kind of faith all my life, the most significant being my own mother. Having been taken away as a child from her original source of support, her family, in an evacuation during World War II, her entire life's journey has been to connect with a higher source of support. It has been my greatest gift in life to observe her journey and learn from her process. She ceaselessly demonstrates the power of Spirit as it moves through our crown and into our lives, paving the way for miracle after miracle. As my mother says, "When we put on our crown, we get out of our own way and allow God to work for us."

When we experience the opening of our crown chakra, the focus of our life shifts from survival to one of infinite possibility. We realize, beyond question, that we are agents of Divine Spirit and our only limitation is our imagination. The seventh chakra provides such a profound sense of peace that it calms all of life's ripples, leaving us feeling like a serene lake at sunrise.

I have seen and even experienced firsthand the deep soothing energy of the fully opened seventh chakra. I find words woefully inadequate in the face of the actual experience. It is the equivalent of pulling the screen back on the drama of life and seeing that no matter how intensely we fall into the process of life, behind the process is our spirit, eternally safe and at one with Divine Source.

IS YOUR CROWN OPEN?

	Yes	No	Sometimes
I know certain things to be true without knowing why.	____	____	____
I have a deep sense of faith.	____	____	____
I do not worry very often.	____	____	____
I sense that God is watching over me.	____	____	____
I trust the Divine order of things.	____	____	____
I surrender my life to Divine direction.	____	____	____
I believe the best for me always happens.	____	____	____
I understand all life experiences to have deep purpose.	____	____	____
I believe that life is not a random event.	____	____	____
I am always open for the Universe to handle things in my life.	____	____	____
I believe in miracles.	____	____	____
I believe all is well no matter how it appears.	____	____	____
I follow my guidance even when it doesn't make sense.	____	____	____

If you answered no to any one of these statements, your crown is not completely open. If you answered no to two or three statements, your crown chakra is fairly open, so to awaken it even further, follow the suggestions for a fairly open crown at the end of the chapter. If you answered no to four to six statements, then your crown is partially open, so to open it up even more, you should follow the suggestions for a partially open crown. If you answered no to seven or more of these statements, then your crown is barely open. To help you move into spiritual expansion and feel the loving return to your Creator, you should follow the suggestions for a closed crown.

SOUL MEMORIES

One of the functions of our crown center is to activate our soul memory, giving us access to the feeling that we have lived before, even if we don't have full memories of past lives and experiences. When we access this direct soul memory, we cannot help but come to regard ourselves as spiritual travelers on a long journey back to Source, God. Having been soul travelers over many lifetimes, we tend to reconnect with those with whom we have unfinished business. Our spiritual assignment is to become unconditionally loving human beings. It isn't much of a challenge to the soul to love those who are agreeable to us. The real opportunity for soul growth comes when we're asked to love someone who is uncooperative. To love someone like this without becoming a slave, a doormat, or a caretaker is a real challenge, and to achieve it is a real victory. Because such victories are so difficult, it may take us several lifetimes to master this ability. That is why we encounter the same people again and again, lifetime after lifetime. We are works in progress, and they are our teachers.

I've had exciting moments in my own life where I felt my crown open to reveal perfect recollections of relationships from past lives with people who are playing a role in my life today. For example, I had dreams of my husband Patrick for a year before I met him. In these dreams, I saw us in a palace in Egypt overlooking the desert, speaking to very large crowds of people. This recurring dream perplexed me, and yet the minute I laid eyes on Patrick for the first time, I knew he was the person I had been dreaming about all along.

Past-life recollections are interesting, even amusing, and they help make sense out of our relationships, especially when they are very painful. But we do not need them to continue the learning process. When we do have them, they strengthen our recognition that all of life, with its relationships and challenges, makes perfect sense to our souls. They remind us that we are not victims of anything. In fact, once the crown opens, we come to know that everything in our life exists by design for the purpose of our growth, and that nothing we face is greater than our capacity to live through and learn from life.

You may have had your own crown-awakening experiences, when you felt drawn to someone as though your destinies were meant to cross. The attraction may be nothing more than a fleeting notion or a pleasant familiarity that you cannot explain. At other times, the feeling may be intense, even life altering. No matter—these reunions do not happen by accident. We are simply picking up where we left off and continuing the learning experience together.

One client for whom I did an intuitive reading told me of her sudden and overwhelming desire to go to Machu Picchu, a temple site in Peru. "When the thought first came to me, I laughed at it because Machu Picchu wasn't even appealing," she said. "I thought the idea was silly. For someone like me, an investment banker who likes vacationing at Club Med, the idea seemed awfully 'New Agey.' And yet it wouldn't go away. The real bizarre twist was that I went to a cocktail party for a fund-raiser for the Metropolitan Museum of Art—and won a trip to anywhere in South America on a raffle. That was too much. Apparently the Universe was trying to tell me that I was supposed to go to Machu Picchu and was so insistent, it even provided the ticket. So I arranged the trip the next day. The minute I showed up for the tour and saw the leader, a good-looking fellow in his late forties, I was overwhelmed with a sense of déjà vu. I couldn't take my eyes off him. It wasn't even a sexual attraction so much as a feeling of 'I know this guy!' He must have had the same feeling because I caught him staring at me, too."

My client continued, "During the course of the next two weeks, the feeling grew even stronger between us, and I had the craziest notion that we had been married in a past life and that our meeting was destined. It wasn't love. It wasn't even lust. We were simply supposed to connect in some way. During the course of the trip, he told me his life's dream about bringing archaeologists and scientists into the area for study and to help the local people pull themselves out of poverty, and how he was having so much trouble raising funds. As for me, I loved Machu Picchu and had an instant rapport with the people. I loved them and his ideas so much that I offered to help out, using my investment background to raise money. That was our connection. We went into business together and have been working hard at this project ever since. It is a struggle, but in it I found a purpose. Whether my instincts about knowing him in a past life are accurate or not, it doesn't really matter. Maybe they are just romantic notions. But I do know that I had an appointment with him on a spiritual level, and that I am completely grateful for the way our venture unfolded. Nothing has ever been more rewarding or come together in such a divinely orchestrated way."

Do you have any recollection of your past lives? What are they?

_____

_____

Do you feel a past-life connection with anyone in your life today? Who?

_____

Even if you cannot recall a past life, are there any specific periods in history or specific places that call to your spirit in a deep and profound way? When? Where?

_____

_____

Do you feel a deeply spiritual connection with any particular person in your life at the moment or in the past?

_____

_____

What spiritual lessons is the Universe teaching you at the moment?

_____

_____

_____

_____

FOLLOWING YOUR PATH

When our crown opens, we find ourselves motivated to do more in life than merely meet our needs. The crown chakra activates our memory of our soul's plan for this life and animates us to actively pursue it.

Every soul comes into this life with a desire for growth, for lessons to learn, patterns to break, and most important, for contributions to make to bring about the greater good for all. Until we activate our crown, these intentions remain dormant and our lives remain focused on more subjective interests driven by learned behavior and acquired beliefs. When we spiritually mature, however, and the crown chakra opens up, we are no longer satisfied with living in such an unconscious way. We begin to desire a more authentic life. We want to leave a more lasting and meaningful impression on the planet. If we do not make choices that align with our higher purpose, we become unbearably restless and desire fundamental change. The urge for soul correction is so great that almost nothing can stop it. This explains why seemingly settled people suddenly become deeply discontented. If their lives aren't supporting their intentions on a soul level, it isn't unusual for them to make a profound change. They may also spontaneously experience unexplained connections of a soulful nature.

If the conditions of your life conflict with your deeper purpose, chances are those conditions will fall by the wayside. This is your soul reminding you of the direction you chose to follow before you came to Earth. You can, of course, always ignore these callings, because you have free will. But those who ignore them often develop a low-grade soul disease of discontent, arising from the lack of harmony between their own energy field and their soul. If you do listen to your wake-up calls from the Universe, however, they will lead you into the greatest and most fulfilling adventures of your life. This is because when the soul calls, the entire Universe is conspiring for your success, if only you answer the call.

My sister Cuky had such a soul-compelling call from the Universe when she was forty-eight years old. She was a flight attendant at the time, living in one of the nicest communities in America, happily married, with two teenage kids at home and a part-time business on the side. By all measures of the American dream, she had it all—except that she felt chronically restless and empty inside. We talked about her emptiness over the years, and she was always open to receiving inspiration. I just kept telling her that timing would play a big role in her finding direction, which seemed to help but didn't make her restlessness any easier.

Things changed when an accident on an airplane left her with a severe knee injury that required surgery. For the first time in her life, she was totally incapacitated, as she lay in bed for weeks recovering from the operation. She finally did recover, only to reinjure the same leg again ten months later. Once again thrown off her feet, she suffered a great deal of pain, and even worse, she feared that she would never walk again.

Because it was hard for me to be objective when she was suffering so much, I referred her to another spiritual healer. When she saw him, she asked, "Why is this happening to me? I don't understand." He answered her, "It's because you are being redirected. You are not following your soul path, and your spirit is trying to help you correct your course."

"What am I supposed to do?" she cried. He said, "You are a healer. Even though you help people through your regular jobs, you have far greater gifts to offer."

"But what should I do? I don't know a thing about healing," she protested.

"Go to school," he said, "and learn about the body. When you do, you'll remember how to heal."

When he suggested that she go to school, something in her said, *Yes! That's it.* She immediately signed up for massage therapy school. There she learned about an ancient Hawaiian healing practice called Lomi Lomi. The minute she heard of this form of massage healing, she got chills. She had loved Hawaii ever since her first visit there, and she returned year after year, never tiring of it. When she heard about Lomi Lomi, she felt as though she were having a past-life memory, as though she had been Hawaiian herself in a past life. A sacred Hawaiian kahuna healing massage, Lomi Lomi is actually a method of soul retrieval for those who have suffered grave psychic injury. To learn the technique, one must apprentice with an authentic Hawaiian kahuna; the teacher to whom Cuky applied was, at eighty-three years old, the last in a line of Hawaiian healers, and she accepted only twelve students out of hundreds of applicants. My sister had the honor of being accepted, and today she is one of only a handful of therapists in America trained by a true Hawaiian kahuna in this very unique form of massage. She has helped anorexics, incest victims, accident victims, drug addicts in recovery, and those she calls "everyday warriors"—people who save lives in their own quiet way. Cuky's clients are lined up from here to Seattle and back; her leg and foot are completely healed, and she is filled with the sense that she is on her true path.

This is an example of the crown chakra opening up, giving someone the courage to break with convention, overcome objections, and follow their heart's desire, no matter how unreasonable or impractical or outrageous it may seem. The crown helps us rise above the mundane in life. It is the center of awareness that says, "Don't settle for less than you are. Remember your spirit, remember your vision, and connect with the heavens to help you see it through."

Have you been feeling restless for meaning in your life?

_____

_____

Have you ever changed your course to pursue a calling?

_____

_____

What obstacles and what opposition stand between you and your true purpose?

_____

_____

Have you answered your calling as of now?

_____

_____

Have you prayed for your calling to reveal itself to you?

_____

_____

Don't worry if you haven't felt a calling yet. We all have our moment, and we all get our orders from God. No one is left out.

TRY THIS!

Energizing Waters

Place a glass of water in a window, and allow it to become energized with the first rays of the morning sun. As soon as you wake up in the morning, drink this water while telling yourself that it represents the loving force of Divine Spirit renewing your body. Imagine, as you drink, that this energized water is cleansing away all debris and psychic pollution, leaving you clear and vitalized for the day ahead.

TRY THIS!

Pray

Just before going to sleep, and upon first waking in the morning, before you even open your eyes, silently pray to your Creator. Ask the Universe to reveal your true calling in life, or if you have already received this guidance, pray that the Universe will give you the energy, courage, and faithfulness necessary to follow it.

SHAKING IT UP

I believe that the desire to experience more in life is often activated by a newly awakened crown chakra and is at the root of many midlife crises. Perhaps it is because by middle age we have achieved enough material security to leave behind the anxieties associated with the lower chakras. Maybe it is because we realize that we are getting older and that the future we have always dreamed of will not come unless we create it. Maybe it is because our spirits get tired of waiting.

The reasons for this psychic restlessness aren't as important as our need to follow its calling. When they experience this activation of the crown chakra, many people make the mistake of thinking they must start all over again, often divorcing spouses, quitting jobs, and seeking to retrieve their youth. But we needn't necessarily dump our current life so much as end our unsatisfying, phony, or unrewarding relationship with it.

This may require that we confront our stale relationships, challenge ourselves to develop our latent talents, or answer the call to personal growth we had forgone earlier in life in order to build our security. Some relationships may end at this time, especially if two people have no authentic connection other than convenience or survival, while others simply require an overhaul. Some may have to quit their job, while others may add an avocation.

In spite of any urge to have a midlife affair, this is less a time to pursue romantic interests than a time to seek a deeper, more meaningful connection with yourself. Often people avoid this invitation to go inward and instead seek to fill their void with outward forms of excitement, completely missing the opportunity to gain the insights to self that lead to inner peace. This is not to suggest that new relationships aren't valuable or shouldn't happen. In fact, it is often an unexpected relationship that activates a dormant crown chakra in the first place. But even though others may facilitate our growth, the relationship we are being called to at this time in our life is with our Creator.

An open crown compels us to know ourselves deeply. It activates our awareness that until everyone on this planet is honored as a spiritual being, there will be no peace or safety on Earth. Life shifts from the drive to get what we can to what we can give back. We all have a contract with our Creator to serve the Universe, and if we have not yet entered into this contract, now as the seventh chakra opens, we will feel compelled to do so.

Part of our service is to offer unconditional love. It is our creative contribution to the planet, our gift to others. Because it comes from our soul, the effort of service is its own reward. We know we are fulfilling our purpose when we find ourselves doing something we love so much that we lose ourselves in it and feel joyful. If you haven't yet experienced your crown awakening into service, don't worry. It may not be time. Some people enter into service at a young age; others when they are senior citizens. On a soul level, you have already scheduled the "what" and "when" of your soul's journey. Your crown will be activated one day by your own restlessness to seek higher ground. Trust that it will. It is the very reason your soul has made the journey into this lifetime.

Have you experienced a midlife crisis or any life crisis?

_____

_____

Are you in search of meaning? In what way have you attempted to find answers and direction?

_____

_____

Have you had any crown-opening experiences? What happened? How did you change afterward?

_____

_____

What kind of service have you offered to the planet?

_____

What purpose have you shared or do you want to share with others?

_____

 TRY THIS!

Breathe

Nothing centers you in your crown chakra more quickly than focusing on your breath. When you breathe steadily and deeply into your body, as opposed to taking tiny shallow half-breaths, you invite your spirit to expand fully into your awareness and you immediately calm the troubled waters of your emotions. When we are upset, the first thing we usually do is hold our breath. The act of calm deep breathing relieves tension, restores us to calm, expands our awareness, and accesses us to Higher Power immediately.

HEALING OUR SPIRIT

The crown chakra serves to unite us with Divine Spirit. We become psychically wounded when we are separated from God. Spiritual healing is the act of reconnecting to the flow of Universal life force and the Divine plan. When the crown chakra opens, this healing allows us to receive the full support of the Universe.

When this happens, we not only heal ourselves but our very presence becomes healing to others. I witnessed a perfect example of this the other day while waiting in the airport to pick up a friend. The plane was delayed, the airport was extremely crowded, and people seemed stressed, anxious, and out of control. You could tell that they were cut off from Spirit by their grim faces, their rude intolerance of one another, and their angry conversations. All, that is, except a two-year-old baby boy who was traveling with his mother. He was oblivious to the tension and was having a perfectly delightful time watching everyone in the waiting area. A friendly child who must have been a very old soul, he walked from person to person as far as his mother would let him wander, catching everyone's eye and then making the silliest face he could until each one laughed. There was nothing shy about this kid or his intentions. One by one he'd pick his target, get right up close, and begin his antics, not budging until he got a laugh. Just a smile wouldn't do. He went for the guffaw! After a few successes, he began to gain an audience, and pretty soon he was getting applause for his efforts. It was absolutely hilarious. The most wonderful part was that he was intentionally cheering up this crowd, even though he was only a baby. And he succeeded. His energy was so alive, so vibrant, and so unabashedly unselfconscious that pretty soon the whole area seemed to take on a new tone. Dark looks disappeared, tight lips eased, and the general aura of the place improved significantly. A baby healed many people that night. It was amazing and humbling to watch.

Spiritual healing may sound rather exotic, something that only very holy or evolved people can do. The truth is, spiritual healing comes naturally to all of us, and it is achieved every time we ground ourselves in our bodies, celebrate our vitality, take ownership of our power, open our hearts, speak our truth, see the beauty in all things, and desire to share this energy with those around us. In other words, we achieve spiritual healing when we are balanced in all of our seven energy centers.

One needn't have any specific training in order to be a healing force in this world. One of the most touching and healing moments of my life occurred spontaneously and continues to have a lasting effect on my heart to this day. I had just finished teaching a workshop in Athens, where I had addressed the most open-hearted and appreciative audience I believe I've ever had. After the talk, I was saying good-bye to the people one at a time when a very beautiful young woman came up to me. "Thank you so much for sharing your heart with me," she said. "I love you so much for your inspiring words. I very much want to give you something to take into your heart, but I am not able to offer you a worthy present. Would you mind if I sang you an old Greek love ballad as an act of appreciation?"

Of course I said I would love it. Completely taken by her clear and pure intention, I sat and listened as she sang me a soulful song in the most beautiful voice I could ever imagine. The entire experience gave me goose bumps and made me cry. Her song healed all the rough edges and fragile places in my heart in an instant. It was like salve on wounds I didn't even know I had! The combination of her voice, her open heart, and her intention to heal me affected me profoundly. To this day I am certain that Heaven sent an angel to sing to me.

No matter who is doing the healing, whether it is a Hawaiian master, a Greek angel, or a two-year-old baby, the essence is the same. The healing force is love, offered with the highest intention and founded on the truth that under it all we are one at heart. Knowing this, you too can become a healer. You may have already served God as an agent of healing energy. You've done it every time you laughed something off instead of becoming enraged. You've done it when you've shared what you love most with others. You've done it when you've offered a kind word or given freely of yourself when it was difficult to do. You've healed when you've restored the confidence of others, believed in their worth even when they doubted themselves, and kept your intention to care for them steady and strong. I believe we all have a lot more "heal" in us than "heel." I believe our crown chakras are more expansive than we recognize. If we would only trust our magnificence, our crown chakras would shine even brighter in our lives.

Have you ever had a healing experience? What happened?

_____

_____

_____

Have you ever sent someone healing thoughts and energy?

_____

_____

Have you ever met a person who has had a healing effect on you?

_____

_____

Has anyone ever suggested that you have a healing effect on him?

_____

If so, were you aware of it? Was it intentional or spontaneous?

_____

_____

SPONTANEOUS AWAKENINGS

The crown chakra can awaken spontaneously. This is not unusual; it happens all the time, but people are reluctant to talk about it. Sometimes the crown chakra opens when people suffer a near-death experience. In these experiences, they feel themselves lifted out of the physical body, feel a sudden and absolute bliss, see a brilliant white light, and feel that they were in some heavenly realm.

I had just such a near-death experience last spring, when I was involved in a car accident with my sister in Kansas City. A car ran a stop sign at full speed and plowed into the side of our car. I distinctly remember that at the moment we were hit, I popped out of my body, and as I did, I thought, "Oh, so this is what death is like. It's not painful at all." A white light totally surrounded me, and I was completely at peace. Suddenly I heard my name being called, and I was instantly back in my body. The air bag had exploded in my face, and black smoke poured out from the engine. My sister freed herself and ran around to my side and pulled the door open like the bionic woman. I turned to the backseat and pulled my niece out. We all crawled out and lay on the ground until the fire trucks came. Miraculously, we were all okay, including the driver of the other car. And it was a great experience, because in that split second, I had a glimpse of what death was like. It was Heaven, just as some say. What a lesson!

Near-death stories are almost identical in reporting that one has little desire to return to the body. If the soul journey is incomplete, however, we must return. Apparently that was the case for me. At the time, I thought I had had an exceptional experience, but since then I have learned that thousands of people have had similar experiences. The last reported statistics suggest that more than 300,000 people worldwide have had near-death soul experiences. These are most definitely crown experiences. They don't occur only on the brink of death, but when they are on this brink, we become conscious that there is more to life than appearances.

Have you ever had a near-death experience? Or have you known anyone who has?

_____

_____

What was your/their experience?

_____

_____

Have you known someone who was dying?

_____

_____

What was your experience?

_____

What did you learn from it?

_____

_____

PRAYER AND MEDITATION

The most effective way to awaken your crown chakra is through the daily practice of prayer and meditation. Prayer is the act of asking for help and guidance in your life. There is no real prescription for prayer. Our personal communication with our Creator is as unique as our fingerprints or the sound of our voice. Each prayer sent is the equivalent of a song sent to heaven. God hears them all. Prayer is most effective, however, when expressed on the deepest level of sincerity, with the intention of turning the control of our lives over to a power greater than ourselves.

I pray in order to have an ongoing dialogue with God. I consider God to be a loving Force. God, as I understand Him, is accessible, healing, and benevolent. Some people avoid prayer because they have learned to perceive God as an angry and punitive force, shaming, unforgiving, ready to banish them to eternal damnation for the sin of being human. Unfortunately, such zealous ideas have distanced many people from the most important loving connection they can have. Usually, no matter how estranged they have become, some life situation will occur that invites them back into a connection with Spirit. Many people will readily attest that without that connection, they would have succumbed to hopelessness and despair.

Meditation is equally important in helping us awaken our seventh chakra. Meditation helps calm our mental chatter and raise our awareness high enough to perceive our Source. Meditation, like prayer, is a matter of personal style. If you find meditating to be difficult, then you might have more positive results if you experiment to find what works best for you.

The most common way to meditate is to focus on the breath, breathing in gently to the count of four and then breathing out gently to the count of four, continuing to do so for ten to fifteen minutes. It is best to gradually work up to it and not force yourself in any way. Avoid letting your mind wander into the future or the past; when it does, gently bring it back to your breath.

If this method doesn't seem to work for you, then you can try repeating a specific mantra, such as "I am at peace" or "I am calm" for the same amount of time. If your body refuses to stay still and you feel very restless, you can try walking meditation, in which you simply focus on walking and nothing else for ten to twenty minutes. You may also want to practice mindful meditation, which is the art of giving your full attention to whatever you are doing as you are doing it and thinking of nothing else.

Meditation, like prayer, has a certain mystique about it that is totally misleading. It takes no talent to meditate, and it isn't intended to affect you like a drug, knocking you out and leaving you unconscious. Meditation as it was taught to me is like taking a cool drink when you are very thirsty. It addresses the thirst of your soul; it nurtures your spirit. Meditation is helpful in managing stress, clearing your mind, calming your emotions, and relaxing your body. It doesn't take much time, it's portable, and it's free. The only requirement is that you do it on a regular basis so that you can begin to feel the benefits. Like exercise, its effects are cumulative. The more you do it, the more you will feel the rewards.

The most important point to make about either praying or meditating is that both are efforts to connect with Spirit. They will leave you refreshed, renewed, and reenergized. These are not assignments to get more spiritual. These are opportunities to appreciate how beautifully spiritual you already are.

Do you pray?

_____

_____

What is your way of praying?

_____

_____

What are you most grateful for?

_____

_____

Do you meditate?

_____

_____

When is your favorite time to meditate?

_____

_____

What are your greatest challenges to meditating?

_____

_____

TRY THIS!

Create a Place to Pray

The act of prayer is very powerful. It becomes even more so when we find or create a special place for prayer. I have several special places where I go to pray. One is the Catholic church in my neighborhood. I love to sit inside when it's quiet and no one else is there. I also love to light the votive candles as a special intention of sending light to those I love. Your prayer place may be outdoors; it may be a quiet corner in your home, or even a public library or museum. It doesn't so much matter where you pray as that your special place is consistent. Then it will take on an energetic charge of its own, and the minute you enter into the space, you will instantly travel to your seventh chakra.

ESCAPISM

Though it is unusual, I do feel it is important to note that people sometimes attempt to awaken their seventh chakra in order to escape their earthly experience. These are people who meditate for hours on end while avoiding the experiences of life. They may form elitist beliefs around their practice and feel spiritually superior to those around them. Others may feel they are spiritually superior because they have read endless numbers of spiritual books. I find this kind of spiritual indulgence another form of addiction. It has the same isolating effects as any other addiction. The number of hours you meditate, the number of workshops you attend, and the number of New Age thinkers and writers you can quote do not measure your connection to Spirit. Spiritual snobbery is just another way the ego tries to run our lives rather than surrender our direction to God.

The simplest way to tune into Spirit and avoid spiritual elitism is to be loving and kind. This means beginning with yourself. When you find yourself shifting from a "me against the world" point to "me as part of the world, and an important part at that," then you are well on your way to leading an enlightened life.

Do you have any desire to "check out"?

_____

_____

_____

Are you guilty of being a spiritual snob, acting as though you are more spiritual than those around you?

_____

_____

_____

GRACE

The best way to become fully aware of the presence of Divine Spirit is to live every day as if it were the holiest day of your life. Try to appreciate the gift of simply being alive. Do everything as if you were doing it as a loving act for your Creator, just as Jesus Christ said, "Whatever you do for the least of my brothers, that you do unto me." When you live life in this truth, you awaken the wisest, most healing, and powerful self that you are. You will experience a life that flows in harmony with the whole.

Living with such loving awareness removes all the obstacles in life and frees your spirit to soar. It is a challenge for even the most committed of spiritual aspirants, so do not set yourself up for failure. Approach your spiritual practice gradually, trying to exercise this point of view for ten minutes a day at the beginning. Work up from there. Strive to live in an awakened and loving state for a day, then two, then more. Keep at it until it becomes a matter of habit, a way of life. To do so will open your seventh chakra, and your life will fill with grace. Events will flow like running water, and you will feel the hand of God in all of your affairs. To live like this simplifies your life. You no longer have to worry about every little detail and can simply look up and enjoy the process. Life then takes on all the beauty the prophets and mystics have seen before us. Awakening your seventh chakra returns to you your innate and infallible knowledge that all is well. You will fully remember that you are a Divine child of the Universe and that your earthly experience is intended to be one of creative and loving joy. This is the final shift in your journey.

What has been the most joyful part of your life?

_____

_____

What would you like to contribute to the world in your life?

_____

_____

 TRY THIS!

Commit to a Spiritual Practice

One of the best ways to open the crown chakra is to commit to a daily spiritual practice. This can be praying or meditating in the morning, tithing those who help you, or offering your services to the community on a regular basis. You know the degree to which you can orient your life toward the spiritual. Start out simply, and build up from there.

BALANCING YOUR CROWN

When your crown is *fairly well* open

- Look for the sacred.

- Listen to Mozart and Gregorian chants.

- Meditate in the morning before getting out of bed.

- Say a prayer of thanksgiving before bed every evening.

- Bless your food before eating.

- Recycle and avoid waste and polluting.

- Wear a spiritual talisman.

- Learn to sing ancient spiritual chants.

- Make up a story about your past life.

- Attend services at a church, mosque, or temple, or visit an ashram.

- Be kind to your family, even when you've had a bad day.

- Participate in a spiritual celebration such as Easter, Passover, Ramadan, the Chinese New Year, or the Summer Solstice.

When your crown is *partially* open

- Consciously bless yourself: The first thing in the morning, before you open your eyes, take in a deep breath, and thank God for giving you one more day to enjoy this beautiful planet.

- Sound a bell to remind yourself to think of Spirit.

- Donate food to the poor.

- Send healing thoughts to someone you love.

- Rent the movie *Little Buddha* by Bernardo Bertolucci.

- Go on a fast.

- Visit the elderly or the ill.

- Talk to God.

- Light a perpetual candle with a specific intention of prayer.

- Give yourself a violet orchid plant to remind you of your own beautiful spirit.

- Meditate regularly.

When your crown chakra is *closed*

- Go on a spiritual pilgrimage to a sacred place.

- Write your own prayers.

- Write to your Higher Self, asking for guidance toward the proper path, and then allow your spirit to respond by writing a reply with your nondominant hand.

- Offer your services to a world emergency organization.

- Build a house in the Habitat for Humanity program.

- Volunteer with others to clean up a toxic site.

- Read the scriptures of a holy tradition.

- Take one day a week off to rest.

- Join a spiritual community.

- Be kind to yourself and others as a spiritual practice.

- Go on a retreat to a monastery or retreat center.

- Sponsor a child in a third-world country.

- Foster parent a child in your community.

- Be a "big brother" or "big sister" to a disadvantaged youth.

- Take up a spiritual practice that supports your beliefs, such as saying the rosary, reading the Koran, or observing the Sabbath.

- Adopt an animal from an animal shelter, and nurse it back to health, especially if you don't relate well to people.

- Offer to coach an inner-city sports team.

- Volunteer for Meals on Wheels, and deliver food to the sick and homebound.

- Begin a prayer wheel with friends.

- Forgive everyone, including yourself!

☼ TRY THIS!

Walk in Beauty

A marvelous Navajo tradition that I use to reconnect with Divine Spirit is to take a Walk in Beauty. To do this, invoke the Universe, ask God to walk with you, and bless every step of your journey with grace.

Suggest to yourself:

May the beauty of Divine Spirit be above me

May the beauty of Divine Spirit be below me

May the beauty of Divine Spirit be behind me

May the beauty of Divine Spirit be in front of me

May the beauty of Divine Spirit surround me

May the beauty of Divine Spirit be Me!

As you align all seven of your energy centers, your chakras, you will enter into a wonderful state of true balance, which is as our Creator intended you to be. In such a grounded, vital, sovereign, loving, expressive, visionary, and expansive state of being, you will undoubtedly not only be inspired in many more ways to maintain your own balance, but you will also receive guidance in how to continue to assist the planet in returning to balance as well. Write down all your personal inspirations and ideas below.

_____

_____

_____

_____

A Balanced Life

As you can see, living a balanced life allows us to feel grounded, vital, sovereign, loving, expressive, perceptive, and spiritually guided every moment of our life. Such a life is a joy to live and makes you a joy to be around! It is a life you can expect to have and that you have a Divine right to experience. Don't worry if you feel far from that reality at this moment. Most of us do. This book is offered as a guide to bringing you closer to that glorious reality, but it is important to know that you should use it to achieve progress, not mastery. Being completely balanced in life is an incredible feat. The only living person I know who has even come close to creating that reality is His Holiness, the Dalai Lama, and I'm sure even he has his moments!

As for the rest of us, the balancing act of life is a never-ending challenge. Some days we soar; other days we find ourselves flat on our rear end. The best approach to achieving true balance is to take it day by day and remain patient, realistic, and easygoing in the process. Achieving true balance is not another test that you must master, and approaching it in that spirit only sets you up for frustration. Work instead to master your moments, and you will know that you are succeeding by how much more energized, more alive, and more genuinely yourself you feel along the way. Approach finding true balance more as a spiritual sport, and allow your own profound sense of well-being to be the only measure of success that matters. Some days will be more balanced than others. Some energy centers will be more balanced than others. And it all can and will change again and again. That is the nature of life, growth, and self-discovery.

The most important thing to know, however, is that no matter how off balance you feel, you are never ever alone in your journey back to center. You are a Divine child of the Universe, and God is always available to assist you. Remember then that you can always ask God for help. Simply doing so lets your angels swoop down and gently correct your course.

Enjoy the process of balancing your life. Whether you are "in the groove" or "on tilt," you are made of light, infinitely lovable, and loved. Embrace your journey back to center joyfully, and take it one step at a time. Ultimately, you will find your psychic equilibrium. It will occur when you surrender into your own magnificence and remember who you really are—a truly balanced light being!

I wish you many blessings along the way.

From the balance beam with love,
Sonia

RESOURCES

SCHOOLS, INSTITUTIONS, AND LEARNING CENTERS

Omega Institute for Holistic Studies

At the Omega Institute, you can nurture body, mind, and spirit with wellness vacations, spiritual retreats, and 250 programs for personal and professional development. The Institute's Lakeside campus is located on eighty scenic acres in Hudson Valley, New York. It offers courses for balancing all seven energy centers.

> 260 Lake Drive
> Rhinebeck, NY 12572
> Phone: (914) 266-4444
> Phone toll-free for catalog: (800) 944-1001
> Website: www.omega-inst.org

New York Open Center
Holistic Learning and Culture

The Open Center offers courses for balancing all seven energy centers.

> 83 Spring Street
> New York, NY 10012
> Phone: (212) 219-2527
> E-mail: box@opencenter.org
> Website: www.opencenter.org

Esalen Institute

This alternative educational center is devoted to the exploration of unrealized human potential. A restorative retreat, it is located on twenty-seven acres along the spectacular Big Sur coastline. It offers weekend and five-day workshops, work-scholar programs, and long-term professional training. Among its workshops are courses for balancing all seven energy centers.

> Highway One
> Big Sur, CA 93920
> Phone: (831) 667-3000
> Website: www.esalen.org

Hendricks Institute

This international learning center is focused on the transformational power of conscious relationship and body-centered techniques, such as breathwork and movement. According to Deepak Chopra, M.D.,

"The inner intelligence of the body is the ultimate and supreme genius. Gay and Kathlyn Hendricks show us how to connect with this inner intelligence and discover the secrets to healing, love, intuition and insight." Gay and Kathlyn Hendricks are the internationally known authors of *Conscious Loving* and more than twenty other books on psychology and transformation. Their institute offers excellent courses for balancing foundation (first chakra), vitality (second chakra), sovereignty (third chakra), heart (fourth chakra), and expression (fifth chakra).

> Gay Hendricks, Ph.D., and Kathlyn Hendricks, Ph.D., ADTR
> 1187 Coast Village Road, Suite 1-416
> Montecito, CA 93108
> Phone: (805) 565-1870
> Fax: (805) 962-0563
> Website: www.hendricks.com

Transitions Learning Center (TLC)

TLC's nurturing environment offers the opportunity to discover and integrate into one's lifestyle the study of alternative health, spirituality, creativity, and mind-body awareness. An extension of Transitions Bookstore, it offers author workshops, seminars, and day-long intensives with national authors.

> 1000 W. North Avenue
> Chicago, IL 60622
> Phone: (312) 932-9076
> Bookstore phone: (312) 951-READ
> Website: www.transitionsbookplace.com

Hazelden Center

This nonprofit organization helps people recover from alcoholism and drug addiction. It offers residential and outpatient treatment, programs for families affected by chemical dependency, and training for professionals. It specializes in balancing the second chakra, for those struggling with addiction.

> P.O. Box 11
> Center City, MN 55012
> Phone: (800) 257-7810

IANDS
International Association for Near Death Studies
IANDS focuses on balancing the (fourth chakra) heart and (seventh chakra) crowning glory.

> National office phone: (860) 528-5144
> Chicago office phone (Diane Willis): (847) 251-7270

Institute of Transpersonal Psychology
Spiritual Emergence Network
Christina Grof, Stanislav Grof, M.D.
The Grof Holotropic Breathwork, an experiential psychotherapy technique, is phenomenal for awakening and balancing the (seventh chakra) crowning glory. Write the institute for workshops in your area. The world's foremost authorities on the subject of spiritual emergence, the Grofs draw on years of dramatic personal and professional experience with transformative states to explore spiritual emergencies. They provide insights for those whose personal transformations may at times be bewildering or disorienting.

> 5905 Soquel Drive, Suite 650
> Soquel, CA 95073
> Phone: (408) 464-8261

WORKSHOPS AND MENTORING PROGRAMS

Listed below are some of my favorite energy-balancing workshops (my own included). Each one further enhances our understanding of our energetic anatomy and teaches us how to best care for our spirit. Each, in some way, is life changing and profoundly healing.

The Hoffman Institute
Liza Ingraci, Managing Director
This institute offers a week-long intensive workshop called the Hoffman Quadrinity Process, aimed at identifying and eliminating patterns of self-sabotaging behavior. The workshop frees you from the past and allows you to connect with your spirit. Excellent for balancing foundation (first chakra), sovereignty (third chakra), heart (fourth chakra), expression (fifth chakra), and vision (sixth chakra). It is offered in four locations across the United States and in twelve countries.

> Phone: (800) 506-5253
> Website: www.hoffmaninstitute.org

The ManKind Project
This international men's network enables men and women to live lives of integrity, accountability, and connection to feeling. It is dedicated to improving the quality of life for families and communities. The New Warrior Training, an intense training adventure weekend and an eight-week integration training, challenges men to look at all aspects of their lives and create new ways of living. Women Within, part of the ManKind Project, offers a program for women comparable to the New Warrior Training. Both are fantastic for balancing the foundation (first chakra), sovereignty (third chakra), heart (fourth chakra), and expression (fifth chakra) in a safe, sane, supportive, and ongoing way.

> Phone: (847) 332-2188
> New Warrior Training: (800) 870-4611
> Women Within: (800) 732-0890

Psychic Pathway Workshop
A three-to-five-day workshop based on my book *The Psychic Pathway,* this workshop introduces you to your natural intuitive voice, while eliminating the blocks that prevent you from hearing the guiding wisdom of your soul. Experientially, you will be introduced to clairvoyance, telepathy, psychometry, your angels and guides, and ultimately to your own Divine spirit. Exciting, empowering, and healing! Reclaim the missing piece, and free your spirit in this life. The workshop balances vitality (second chakra), heart (fourth chakra), expression (fifth chakra), and vision (sixth chakra).

> Inner Wisdom, Inc.
> P.O. Box 408996
> Chicago, IL 60640
> Phone: (773) 989-1151
> E-mail: inrwisdom@aol.com
> Website: www.inner-wisdom.com

Translucent You! Workshop
This joyful five-day "camp for the soul" with my sister, Cuky Choquette Harvey,

and me, will bring complete rejuvenation of mind, body, and spirit in the glorious background of Kauai, Hawaii. I will be mentoring you through daily coursework on energetic balance, and Cuky through physical renewal rituals and therapies. Together, along with healers in cranial sacral, body mechanics, and sound and dance therapy, we will experience a profound vibrational shift from ordinary consciousness into a heightened state of awareness that can only be described accurately as Translucent You! It balances all seven chakras in the most joyful and sensual way! To register or for information, contact Cuky.

13240 Barkley Street
Overland Park, KS 66209
Phone: (913) 681-5602
Fax: (913) 851-8336

Avatar Training
Steven Hartman
Certified Avatar Master, Facilitator

Avatar is a life-changing nine-day course on the mechanics of beliefs, creativity, and tapping into personal power. Steven is a masterful teacher who brings his own gifts of intuition, mentoring, and healing to this already-powerful process. If you are stuck in the muck of life and can't move on, this workshop will get you back on track and into the life you deserve and desire. It is especially effective with foundation (first chakra), sovereignty (third chakra), expression (fifth chakra), and vision (sixth chakra).

Chicago phone: (773) 528-0543

Your Heart's Desire Workshop

This powerful and extremely fun two-day workshop, based on my book *Your Heart's Desire*, is designed to bring the nine principles of *Your Heart's Desire* into reality. Work on each principle along with others in a safe, grounded, and supportive setting as you move intentionally toward creating the life you really want! This workshop will capture your heart and release your full potential to be the powerful creator that you are. It is wonderful for vitality (second chakra), sovereignty (third chakra),

heart (fourth chakra), and expression (fifth chakra).

Inner Wisdom, Inc.
P.O. Box 408996
Chicago, IL 60640
Phone: (773) 989-1151
E-mail: inrwisdom@aol.com
Website: www.inner-wisdom.com

True Balance Workshop

Life can be an energizing and exciting adventure when you are truly balanced. Join me and my team of healers as we introduce you to your own magnificence! This workshop, based on this book, introduces you to each of your seven energy centers; teaches you about their function, how to keep them balanced, and what throws them off balance; and finally, restores them back into balance in practical, familiar, and joyful ways. In a truly balanced state, we naturally tap into our greatest self and become the best that we are designed to be. This is a gift to ourselves and to the world. It is my favorite way to keep all seven chakras balanced!

Inner Wisdom, Inc.
P.O. Box 408996
Chicago, IL 60640
Phone: (773) 989-1151
E-mail: inrwisdom@aol.com
Website: www.inner-wisdom.com

Art Breaks

Annette Tacconelli, an artist, intuitive, and teacher, leads this experiential, art-driven class that uses movement to clear the path, intuition exercises to increase understanding, and art to fuel joy. Blocks are dispersed and creativity is increased in this lively and involved class. It is especially effective for reawakening vitality (second chakra), heart (fourth chakra), expression (fifth chakra), and vision (sixth chakra).

Chicago phone: (773) 381-2522

Don Campbell's Mozart Effect

Don Campbell is a musicologist and author of *The Mozart Effect* and a host of other books and recordings. According to Julia Cameron *(The Artist's Way)*, "Don Campbell is the dean emeritus of sound healers. His work is of inestimable value. Practical, mystical and visionary, he makes the world of music accessible, friendly, and profoundly healing." His work is fantastic for expression (fifth chakra) and crowning glory (seventh chakra).

> The Mozart Effect Resource Center
> 3526 Washington Avenue
> St. Louis, MO 63103-1019
> Phone: (800) 721-2177
> Fax: (314) 531-8384
> Website: www.mozarteffect.com

Alan Cohen's Mastery Training

The author of many inspirational books, including *Happily Even After* and *A Deep Breath of Life,* Alan teaches spiritual awakening and visionary living seminars throughout the United States and abroad. His seminars are wonderful for balancing the heart (fourth chakra), vision (sixth chakra), and crowning glory and expansion (seventh chakra).

> P.O. Box 5100
> Carlsbad, CA 92018-5100
> or
> Alan Cohen Mastery Training Programs
> 430 Kukuna Road
> Haiku, HI 96708
> Phone: (800) 568-3079
> Website: www.alancohen.com
> Phone for catalog (Hay House): (800) 462-3013

The Artist's Way Workshop

All of us are profoundly creative, and all of us can be far more creative through the use of a few simple tools. Join Julia Cameron, author of *The Artist's Way,* as she teaches the tools of creative recovery. Working from three tool kits drawn from her best-selling books—*The Artist's Way, The Vein of Gold,* and *The Right to Write*—Cameron teaches an eclectic and innovative selection of tools to deepen, expand, and clarify creativity. She has taught and refined her methods for two decades. The creative principles that she articulates will help artists and nonartists alike—anyone interested in living more creatively. Julia is outstanding for her ability to balance vitality (second chakra) and expression (fifth chakra). I attribute my writing career to Julia's talent. She freed my creative voice and empowered me to write, and she can do the same for you. To contact Julia or find out about the workshops, write to:

> Penguin Putnam, Inc.
> 375 Hudson Street
> New York, NY 10014

The Painting Experience

With Stewart Cubley, author of *Life, Paint, Passion: Reclaiming the Magic of Spontaneous Expression* (New York: Tarcher/Putnam,1996). The Painting Experience method views the act of creation as the deepest point of contact with one's essential self, where the process of facing the unknown color, form, and image becomes a vehicle for entering the mystery of one's own being, and a tool for liberation and awakening. In the Life, Paint, and Passion workshops, you undertake a profound journey of free play and self-revelation, experiencing firsthand the flow of intuitive creation along with its potential for transformation, healing, and insight. No prior experience in art is required. All materials are supplied. The workshops are excellent for balancing vitality (second chakra), heart (fourth chakra), expression (fifth chakra), and vision (sixth chakra). Stewart's work is exciting, daring, and tremendously liberating for anyone's imbalanced and bound-up soul.

> Studio for Process Arts
> P.O. Box 309
> Fairfax, CA 94978
> Phone: (415) 455-4682
> Toll-free phone: (888) 639-8569
> Fax: (415) 457-8633
> Website: www.processarts.com

Nightingale-Conant
Your Psychic Pathway Mentoring Program

In this program, based on the audiocassette program *Your Psychic Pathway,* a gifted, practiced intuitive mentors you in a series of one-on-one telephone consultations into your own intuitive power, and helps you apply this newly reclaimed wisdom to your life. It is especially appealing and effective for people who desire to become intuitive healers and practitioners themselves. It is also excellent for balancing foundation (first chakra), sovereignty (third chakra), heart (fourth chakra), expression (fifth chakra), and vision (sixth chakra).

    Phone: (800) 323-5552

The Wise Child Workshop
Learn to nurture your intuition and creativity at home! This three-to-five-day workshop, based on my book *The Wise Child,* is designed to reawaken intuition in your family. Create an intuition-friendly atmosphere in your home, one that recognizes all family members as precious, enlightened spiritual beings who are naturally guided by spirit. The workshop is great for balancing foundation (first chakra), sovereignty (third chakra), heart (fourth chakra), expression (fifth chakra), and vision (sixth chakra).

    Inner Wisdom, Inc.
    P.O. Box 408996
    Chicago, IL 60640
    Phone: (773) 989-1151
    E-mail: inrwisdom@aol.com
    Website: www.inner-wisdom.com

The Baniel Feldenkrais System
This revolutionary new approach accesses the body's own intelligence to bring about increased mobility, vitality, well-being, freedom from pain, and balance between the physical, mental, and spiritual. Anat Baniel, a master teacher of the method, works worldwide with musicians, athletes, babies, the elderly, and the general public. The system specializes in balancing foundation (first chakra) and sovereignty (third chakra).

    Anat Baniel
    336 Bon Air Center, No. 384
    Greenbrae, CA 94904
    Phone: (415) 464-0777
    Toll-free phone: (800) 386-1441
    Fax: (415) 464-0779
    E-mail: anatbaniel@feldenkrais-intl.com
    Website: www.feldenkrais-intl.com

Fairy Tales, Inc.
Laura DeRocher
Dream Fulfillment Performing Art Camp
Work with a team of kindly wizards and fairy godmothers trained in theater arts and in Heart's Desire manifestation principles to craft your own personal fairy tale. In a playful and safe theater environment, slay your own personal dragons and crystallize your dreams, wish them out into the Universe, then watch them come true in a live theatrical, musical, or dance performance crafted by you for you. Take home a videotape to reinforce the happy ending you are creating.

    E-mail: DerocherL@aol.com
    Website: lauraderocher.com

LOCAL GROUPS

Listed below are valuable groups available in most local areas. Each is designed to assist you in finding your balance. All are free of charge and provide ongoing support and personal friendship and guidance.

    Alcoholics Anonymous
    Website: www.alcoholicsanonymous.org

    Al-Anon Family Group Headquarters
    Website: www.al-anon.alateen.org

    Overeaters Anonymous
    Website: www.overeatersanonymous.org

    Debtors Anonymous
    Website: www.debtorsanonymous.org

These groups are listed in your local telephone directory. Once you attend a meeting, you will find out about more available groups. Www.12steps.org lists various twelve-step meetings by state and country. Check your local directory for phone listings. All twelve-step groups work to strengthen all seven chakras, but they are particularly helpful to those whose second chakra is moderately to severely out of balance.

Habitat for Humanity

An international nonprofit project uniting volunteers and resources to eliminate poverty housing. Check your local phone directory for listings. Habitat for Humanity is excellent for balancing foundation (first chakra) and heart (fourth chakra).

Website: www.habitat.org

Toastmasters

Toastmasters is a nonprofit organization that helps people speak more effectively and gain leadership skills by organizing and conducting meetings. Its members learn to give impromptu speeches, present prepared speeches, and conduct meetings in a supportive environment. Toastmasters has more than eight thousand clubs worldwide. Look in your local phone directory for a club near you, or call the international organization. This is a terrific way to balance the expression (fifth chakra).

P.O. Box 9052
Mission Viejo, CA 92690
Phone: (949) 858-8255
Toll-free phone: (800) 993-7732
Website: www.toastmasters.org.

A Course In Miracles

Check your area Unity Church for workshops. A Course in Miracles is fabulous for balancing all seven chakras, but it is especially effective for opening the seventh chakra.

PRIVATE PRACTITIONERS

Listed below are my favorite healers, teachers, mentors, and intuitive counselors. Every single one of them, in some deeply meaningful and lasting way, has been a personal healer of mine. I believe each one of these individuals is absolutely capable of assisting you in bringing all your chakras into balance, as they have done for me. With each person's name, I have listed chakra numbers indicating where I believe they do their most empowered work. But that does not mean that they are limited to healing or rebalancing only that particular energy center. Rather, it only suggests a starting point that may

best correspond to your personal imbalances. I am deeply grateful for all they have done for me and am extremely appreciative that they have graciously agreed to be listed in this book so that others may benefit from their gifts as well. I recommend them to you with the greatest respect and enthusiasm.

Patrick Tully, C.M.T. (chakras 1–7)

Cocreator of the Psychic Pathway and Your Heart's Desire workshops and my husband and life partner, Patrick is a master at profound chakra balancing through the use of breathwork, hypnosis, visualization, meditation, and massage therapy. Working through energy blocks, Patrick brings one into alignment—body, mind, and soul—with one's deepest heart's desires. He specializes in helping clients find a sense of purpose and mission, emotional release, and personal rejuvenation. Through combining all his modalities of healing, Patrick is excellent at balancing all seven energy centers and restoring one to true balance!

Chicago phone: (773) 989-2112
Fax: (773) 989-9987

Cuky Choquette Harvey, L.C.M.T. (chakras 1–7)

Apprenticed by a master teacher, my sister Cuky is a profound healer in the art of Lomi Lomi Hawaiian-style massage, a ten-thousand-year-old transformational system of massage therapy originally performed by the kahunas of Hawaii, as well as La Stone therapy, classic traditional bodywork, and soul journeying. Her own unique and powerful healing shakti revitalizes the natural child's spirit and purity held within all of us. An intuitive and clairvoyant, Cuky has an ability to journey into the seven energy centers of the body and identify past injuries. In a joyful and safe setting, she will help you to call your spirit home. She is wonderful if you are depleted, have lost your love of life, or are inclined to self-abuse or neglect. Cuky balances all seven energy centers, but she is especially healing to those who have lost their vitality (second chakra), and those who are ready to move into the next level of real success.

13240 Barkley Street
Overland Park, KS 66209
Phone: (913) 681-5602
Fax: (913) 851-1336

Debra Grace Graves, C.M.T. (chakras 1, 4, 7)

Debra is a highly intuitive bodyworker specializing in cranial-sacral and subtle energy work to eliminate chakra blockages and restore energy. Her touch is very light, but the effects are profound and deeply healing. Debra is also an excellent intuitive reader and life coach and is perfect for those who need psychic support in difficult times of transition. She is available for both bodywork in person and intuitive readings by phone. She is tremendous in her ability to balance foundation (first chakra), heart (fourth chakra), and crowning glory (seventh chakra), and in personal expansion. She helps people move out of their own way and onto their path.

St. Louis phone: (636) 936-8222

LuAnn Glatzmaier, M.A. (chakras 1, 2, 5, 6)

A highly gifted and profound intuitive counselor and one of my own greatest personal mentors, LuAnn is especially talented at helping people discover their calling or purpose in life as well as untangling the difficulties of relationship crises. When you want to get at the "big picture" of why things are happening in your life, she is perfect: she helps you identify your soul lessons in this life. She is especially effective for people who are in crises or who need an intervention to facilitate growth. LuAnn specializes in balancing foundation (first chakra), vitality (second chakra), expression (fifth chakra), and vision (sixth chakra). She does private consultations by phone nationally.

Phone: (303) 394-3056
Fax: (303) 394-3560

Anthony Pinciotti (chakras 1, 2, 5)

A nationally known drummer based in New York, Anthony offers group and individual lessons in traditional and improvisational drumming techniques, incorporating a spiritual approach to music. He is wonderful for balancing foundation (first chakra) and vitality (second chakra), as well as expression (fifth chakra).

Phone: (773) 381-2522
International pager: (888) 990-3219

Joan M. Smith, Astrologer (chakras 1–7)

Joan can provide a fabulous overview of your life path. She addresses all seven chakras on a physical, creative, and spiritual level. She has both "belly" knowledge and cerebral insight. She will give you the best and worst of your life's unfolding, year by year, and she will act as a personal guide through all of your life challenges. Joan will help you to identify which energy centers need special attention each year. She has kept me on track and out of harm's way for more than twenty years. She even foresaw this book years before I did. Joan does private consultations by phone nationally.

1621 Trenton Street
Denver, CO 80220
Phone: (303) 394-3056
Fax: (303) 394-3560

Mark Stanton Welch (chakras 2, 4, 5)

Mark's music is healing, motivational, thought provoking, and empowering and will assist anyone who wants to strengthen his or her personal expression. A talented sound healer, he teaches sound therapy. He composes personal music for individuals and for groups. He is also available for conferences and special events. I have worked with Mark for the past several years and find that his music lifts depression, inspires creativity, and restores joy. Mark is wonderful for supporting vitality (second chakra), heart (fourth chakra), and expression (fifth chakra).

P.O. Box 1331
Cambria, CA
Phone: (805) 927-2416

Anne Simon Wolf, M.S.S.W.
(chakras 1, 2, 3, 5)
Anne is a mentor, coach, and personal guide in reclaiming authority in life. Through her combined intuitive, therapeutic, and mentoring skills, she is by far one of the best life path coaches I've ever known. She is especially effective if you are serious about creating a life that is in harmony and balance with your true essence. She personally helped me to stay true to my spirit when it seemed that everything was conspiring against it, and she led me through one of the darkest periods in my life with a strong and loving hand and with powerful and wise guidance. Anne restores balance to foundation (first chakra), vitality (second chakra), sovereignty (third chakra), and expression (fifth chakra). She is available nationally for coaching and counseling by phone.

> 313 Price Place, Suite 107
> Madison, WI 53705
> Phone: (608) 231-0231

Briah Anson, M.A. (chakras 1, 2, 4)
One of Briah's key strengths is her breadth of experience with complementary modalities. She helps clients by gently guiding them through the Rolfing process, allowing their process to lead the way. She is a certified practitioner with more than twenty years of experience and is the author of *Rolfing: Stories of Personal Empowerment*. Several years ago, Patrick and I were rehabbing our hundred-year-old house. The project was overwhelming and threw my first chakra completely off balance. Briah restored my equilibrium and got me through the worst of it. She is excellent for balancing foundation (first chakra), vitality (second chakra), and heart (fourth chakra).

> St. Paul phone: (651) 228-9569

Annette Tacconelli (chakras 2, 5, 6)
A shaman, artist, intuitive, and teacher, Annette's work consists of neoshamanic healings and intuition and creativity classes. Her classes include Art Breaks, an experiential, art-driven intuition class, and Film Club, which playfully explores the content and ritual of film as a healing modality. If your vitality (second chakra), expression (fifth chakra), or vision (sixth chakra) is not balanced, Annette will come to the rescue in a way that will both delight and heal you. She is one of the most intuitive and gifted teachers I've ever met.

> Chicago phone: (773) 381-2522

Diane Willis (chakras 4, 7)
Diane specializes in supporting people through grief, death, dying, and grief-related issues. She is especially healing to those who are working on unresolved issues with someone who is dying, those who have a family member who has recently died, and those who are overcome with the fear of death. I have found her wisdom, creativity, and passion for sharing the truth and for healing others boundless. She is fabulous for balancing the heart (fourth chakra) and for awakening your crowning glory (seventh chakra). She does consultations nationally by phone.

> Phone: (847) 251-5144

Ken Carlson
Ken Carlson, author of *Starman*, is a wonderful intuitive who works with flower and crystal essences to restore balance in the subtle energy body and the chakra system. Using his intuition he evaluates your chakra system, as well as your emotional body, and then recommends specific flower essences native to Hawaii, or crystal essences from all over the world to bring your spirit back into harmony with your purpose. He is excellent in identifying problems, and his flower essences are the best I've ever used.

> Starmen Unlimited
> P.O. Box 698
> Kilauea, HI 96754

BOOKS AND TAPES

For Your Foundation

Breathnach, Sarah Ban. *Simple Abundance*. New York: Warner Books, 1995.

Craze, Richard. *The Tao of Food*. Los Angeles: Goldfield Press, 1999.

Hay, Louise. *Heal Your Body*. Carlsbad, CA: Hay House, 1994.

Jaynes, Julian. *The Origin of Consciousness in the Breakdown of the Bicameral Mind*. Boston: Houghton Mifflin, 1990.

Kingston, Karen. *Clear Your Clutter with Feng Shui*. New York: Broadway, 1999.

Northrup, Christiane, M.D. *Women's Bodies, Women's Wisdom*. New York: Bantam Books, 1998.

Richmond, Lewis. *Work as a Spiritual Practice*. New York: Broadway, 1999.

For Your Vitality

Anand, Margo. *The Art of Sexual Ecstasy*. New York: Tarcher/Putnam, 1991.

Borysenko, Joan. *Fire in the Soul*. New York: Warner, 1994.

Cameron, Julia. *The Artist's Way*. New York: Tarcher/Putnam, 1992.

Cappachione, Lucia. *The Power of Your Other Hand*. Van Nuys, CA: Newcastle, 1998.

Guy, David. *The Red Thread of Passion*. Boston: Shambhala, 1999.

Moore, Thomas. *Care of the Soul*. New York: HarperPerennial, 1994.

For Your Personal Sovereignty

Allen, James. *As You Think*. Novato, CA: New World Library, 1998.

Artress, Lauren. *Walking a Sacred Path*. New York: Riverhead Books, 1996.

Chodron, Pema. *When Things Fall Apart*. Boston: Shambhala, 1997.

Khan, Hazrat Inayat. *Spiritual Dimensions of Psychology*. New Lebanon, NY: Omega, 1990.

McGraw, Philip. *Life Strategies*. New York: Hyperion, 1999.

Millman, Dan. *The Way of the Peaceful Warrior*. Tiburon, CA: H.J. Kramer, 1985.

Moore, Robert L., and Douglas Gillette. *King, Warrior, Magician, Lover*. San Francisco: Harper San Francisco, 1991.

Wilde, Stuart. *Life Was Never Meant to Be a Struggle*. Carlsbad, CA: Hay House, 1998.

For Your Heart

Caine, Kenneth. *Prayer, Faith and Healing*. Emmaus, PA: Rodale, 1999.

Choquette, Sonia. *Your Heart's Desire*. New York: Three Rivers Press, 1997.

A Course in Miracles, 2nd ed. Foundation for Inner Peace. New York: Viking, 1996.

Kingma, Daphne Rose. *The Future of Love*. Main Street Books, 1999.

Kornfield, Jack. *The Path with Heart*. New York: Bantam, 1993.

Lamott, Anne. *Traveling Mercies*. New York: Pantheon, 1999.

Ruiz, Don Miguel. *The Mastery of Love*. San Rafael, CA: Amber-Allen, 1999.

Nightingale-Conant. *Creating Your Heart's Desire* by Sonia Choquette

This audiocassette workshop program introduces you to the nine steps of creative manifestation and shows you how to use them to bring all your desires into being. Workbook with course materials included. Call (800) 525-9000.

For Your Expression

Burke, James. *Connections*. Boston: Little, Brown, 1995.

Cameron, Julia. *The Right to Write*. New York: Tarcher/Putnam, 1999.

Claxton, Guy. *Hare Brain, Tortoise Mind*. Hopewell, N.J.: Ecco Press, 1999.

Dossey, Larry, M.D. *Healing Words*. New York: HarperCollins, 1995.

Goldberg, Natalie. *Writing Down the Bones*. Boston: Shambhala, 1998.

Kabat-Zinn, Jon. *Wherever You Go, There You Are.* New York: Hyperion, 1995.

Lamott, Anne. *Bird by Bird.* New York: Anchor Books/Doubleday, 1995.

Zubrin, Robert. *Entering Space.* New York: Tarcher/Putnam, 1999.

For Your Personal Vision

Anderson, George, and Andrew Barone. *Lessons from the Light.* New York: Putnam, 1999.

Andrews, Lynn. *The Woman of Wyrrd.* New York: Harper, 1991.

Choquette, Sonia. *The Psychic Pathway.* New York: Three Rivers Press, 1995.

Choquette, Sonia. *The Wise Child.* New York: Crown, 1999.

Coelho, Paulo. *The Alchemist.* New York: HarperCollins, 1995.

Orloff, Judith. *Second Sight.* New York: Warner Books, 1997.

Yogananda, Paramahansa. *Autobiography of a Yogi.* Los Angeles: Self Realization Press, 1997.

Nightingale-Conant. *Your Psychic Pathway*

This audiocasette program reveals an inner wisdom that guides, protects, and inspires you. In a practical and grounded way, you'll learn to access your inner voice and use it to find new opportunities, discover your talents, connect with your spiritual family, and illuminate your life's path. Call (800) 525-9000.

For Your Crowning Glory

Bodine, Echo. *Echoes of the Soul.* Novato, CA: New World Library, 1999.

Das, Lama Surya. *Awakening to the Sacred.* New York: Broadway Books, 1999.

Grey, Alex. *Sacred Mirrors.* Rochester, VT: Inner Traditions International, 1998.

Hanh, Thich Nhat. *Going Home.* New York: Riverhead Books, 1999.

Hanh, Thich Nhat. *The Miracle of Mindfulness.* Boston: Beacon Press, 1999.

Levine, Stephen. *A Year to Live.* New York: Three Rivers Press, 1998.

Newton, Michael, Ph.D. *Journey of Souls.* St. Paul, MN: Llewellyn Publications, 1996.

Praagh, James Van. *Talking to Heaven.* New York: Dutton, 1997.

Walsh, Neale Donald. *Conversations with God, Books 1–3.* New York: Putnam, 1996-98.

Weiss, Brian, M.D. *Many Lives, Many Masters.* New York: Simon & Schuster, 1988.

Zukav, Gary. *The Seat of the Soul.* New York: Simon & Schuster, 1990.